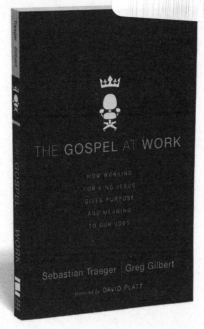

THE GOSPEL AT WORK

HOW WORKING
FOR KING JESUS
GIVES PURPOSE
AND MEANING
TO OUR JOBS

Sebastian Traeger | Greg Gilbert

foreword by DAVID PLATT

We hope you enjoy this complimentary copy of *The Gospel at Work*
by Sebastian Traeger and Greg Gilbert. This book is intended to be
a resource for anyone in your congregation who wonders how the
Gospel impacts their work. Whether they have made an *idol* of work
or find themselves being *idle* at work, *The Gospel at Work* reminds us
all of one crucial life-changing fact: *Who* you work for is infinitely
more important than what you do!

The Gospel at Work is an excellent resource
to use with your congregation as a small
group study and includes a FREE study guide
and curriculum video available online at
thegospelatwork.com/studyguide

THE GOSPEL AT WORK

HOW WORKING
FOR KING JESUS
GIVES PURPOSE
AND MEANING TO OUR JOBS

Sebastian Traeger | Greg Gilbert

foreword by DAVID PLATT

ZONDERVAN®

ZONDERVAN

The Gospel at Work
Copyright © 2013 by James Sebastian Traeger and Gregory D. Gilbert

This title is also available as a Zondervan ebook.
Visit www.zondervan.com/ebooks.

Requests for information should be addressed to:

Zondervan, *Grand Rapids, Michigan* 49530

ISBN: 978-0-310-52279-9 (Special Edition)

All Scripture quotations, unless otherwise indicated, are taken from The Holy Bible, *New International Version®, NIV®*. Copyright © 1973, 1978, 1984, 2011 by Biblica, Inc.® Used by permission. All rights reserved worldwide.

Scripture quotations marked KJV are taken from the King James Version of the Bible.

Any internet addresses (websites, blogs, etc.) and telephone numbers in this book are offered as a resource. They are not intended in any way to be or imply an endorsement by Zondervan, nor does Zondervan vouch for the content of these sites and numbers for the life of this book.

Cover design: Michelle Lenger
Cover images: iStockphoto
Interior design: David Conn

Printed in the United States of America

14 15 16 17 18 19 20 /DCI/ 18 17 16 15 14 13 12 11 10 9 8 7 6 5 4 3 2 1

To my family—Nikki, Alex, Wesley, and Analeigh.
You all are, without a doubt, the greatest blessing and joy
God has given me in this life.
I love you and pray that our lives
will increasingly be lived for the King.

—Sebastian Traeger

To my grandfathers, Ralph Gilbert
and E. W. "Dude" Surratt.
It wasn't with glory or fame but with honor
and faith that they served their King.
Well done, good and faithful servants of Jesus.

—Greg Gilbert

CONTENTS

BY DAVID PLATT

If the people I pastor work forty hours a week for forty years of their lives, that means they will put in more than eighty thousand hours at a job during their lifetime. These hours don't even include the thousands they spend in school preparing for work, on top of thousands more they spend in cars, planes, and trains traveling to work. Consequently, one of our greatest needs in the church is an understanding of how daily work according to God's Word ties in with God's ultimate purpose in the world.

We in the church desperately need to see how God himself delights in work and God himself designed our work by his grace for our good and for his glory. At the same time, we need to see how work, as a mark of human dignity, has been marred by human depravity. Work that was designed to be fulfilling is frustrating; work that was designed to be purposeful feels pointless; and work that was designed to be selfless has become selfish. As a result, we find ourselves on one hand overvaluing work to the neglect of our health, our families, and the church, or on the other hand undervaluing work in a culture that fosters the unbiblical ideal of laziness and glorifies the unbiblical idea of retirement.

But there is another way—a better way—to work, a way that is made possible by the work of Christ on the cross. In the gospel, Christ himself has secured salvation from our sin, satisfaction for our souls, and significance in our work in such a way that we are now free to worship God wholeheartedly as we work, to love others selflessly in our work, and to trust God completely with our work. The gospel brings significant meaning to the seemingly mundane and provides a supreme purpose for every employee and employer on the planet.

For this reason, I am delighted, ecstatic, and overjoyed (and I could go on with more descriptors!) to commend this book to you. As soon as I finished reading *The Gospel at Work* by Sebastian Traeger and Greg Gilbert, my first thought was, "I wish that every single member of the church would read this book." For here a leader in the marketplace and a pastor in the church wonderfully blend biblical foundations with practical implications that I am hopeful, when understood and applied, will mobilize men and women who are working hard at whatever they do for the adornment of the gospel and working strategically wherever God leads for the advancement of the gospel, all to the furtherance of God's fame in the mission field known as the marketplace.

David Platt, Birmingham, Alabama

THE CHALLENGE

If you're like most people, you spend a significant portion of every week of your life at your job. You also spend quite a lot of time *thinking* about your job. What do I need to do next? How do I maximize profit, or how do I solve that problem, or how do I communicate this need?

It may well be that at least some of your thoughts about your job are not just about operations. They're about the meaning of it all. Why am I doing this? What's the purpose of it, and do I want to keep doing it? How is this job affecting me as a human being, making my life better or worse? Is it all worth it, and why?

Those are good questions, of course. But if you're a Christian, there's another set of questions that is even more important—questions that have to do with how your work fits into God's intentions for your life. Is my work shaping my character in a godly direction? How can I do my work, not just as a way to put food on the table, but as a sold-out disciple of Jesus? What's the point of work, anyway, in a Christian's life? Is there any meaning to it beyond providing goods and services, making money, and providing a living for myself and my family? And why, for that matter, does God have us spend so much of our lives doing this one particular thing?

As we've talked with Christians in our own churches and circles of friendship, this concern about the meaning or purpose of work shows up again and again in people's thoughts about their jobs. They want to know how what they do for forty-plus hours a week fits into God's plans. They want to know what purpose it plays, not just in their own lives, but in God's greater intentions for the world. They ask, "This job that takes up so many hours of my life and so much of my mental space, that frustrates me to no end sometimes and gives me great joy at other times—what does it all finally mean?" Those are important questions, and they come from a good and right sense that nothing in our lives, including our jobs, is there simply as "window decoration." It all fits into the great story of creation, sin, and redemption. God has a purpose for all of it.

HOW OUR WORK FITS INTO THE STORY

God's intention, from the very beginning, was for human beings to work. Work is not a result of sin—even though we experience terrible days that tempt us to believe it is! From the moment God created Adam and Eve, he gave them work to do. He made a garden and told them, "Work it and take care of it" (Genesis 2:15). The work Adam and Eve were meant to do was perfectly joyful, perfectly fulfilling work. There was no mindless toil, no cutthroat competition, no sense of futility. They did everything in service to the Lord himself and in perfect relationship to him. Their work was simply a matter of gathering up God's overflowing blessing to them!

Adam and Eve's sin, of course, changed that. When they disobeyed God's command and rebelled against him, work stopped being purely a reaping of God's abundance. Adam's sin and God's curse against it affected the very soil of the ground. Work became painful and necessary for Adam's and Eve's very survival. Where once the earth had eagerly produced its fruit — almost holding it out with eager hands and begging Adam and Eve to take it — now the earth became stingy. It withheld its riches, and the humans were forced to labor hard and painfully to get them. Life east of Eden was wholly different from life inside it.

Understanding that part of the Bible's story and work's place in it is actually crucial for us as Christians, because it helps explain why our work will always, to some degree or another, be marked by frustration. Work is hard because both we and the world around us have been affected by our turning away from God. Because of that, it shouldn't surprise us that work is difficult and painful sometimes. Work has a tendency to wear us out and wear us down. It can be a source of massive frustration in our lives. On the other hand, it shouldn't surprise us that when we *do* enjoy our work, there is an always-present danger that our work will swallow us whole — that our hearts will come to be defined by it and we will be reduced to nothing *but* workers.

Work is necessary, work is hard, and work is even dangerous. For all that, however, it's still clear that God cares deeply about how we think about and relate to our jobs. What you do and how you do it are not uninteresting to him. When Jesus died on the cross and rose from the dead to redeem a people for himself, he also committed to conform them more and more closely to him by the power of the Holy Spirit. The Bible tells us he does that through all the circumstances of our lives — including our jobs. Our jobs are one of the primary ways God intends to make us more like Jesus. He uses our work to sanctify us, develop our Christian character, and teach us to love him more and serve him better until we join him on the last day in resting from our labors.

The New Testament actually makes a pretty big deal of how we should think about our work. The following passages of Scripture are crucial if we're going to have a biblical understanding of our jobs and their purposes in God's plan of redemption.

In Ephesians 6:5, 7, the apostle Paul tells us to perform our jobs "with sincerity of heart, just as you would obey Christ ... Serve wholeheartedly, as if you were serving the Lord, not people." In Colossians 3:22–24, he tells us we should do so "with sincerity of heart and reverence for the Lord." "Whatever you do," Paul goes on to write, "work at it with all your heart, as working for the Lord, not for human masters ... It is the Lord Christ you are serving."

What amazing statements those are! Look more closely at what the Bible says about your job: Whatever you do, you are to do it "*as if you were serving the Lord, not people.*" You are to work "with all your heart, *as working for the Lord and not for human masters.*" Do you see the incredible significance of those phrases? Work is not just a way to pass the time and make money. Your job is actually service that you render *to the Lord himself*!

Do you think about your job like that? Do you realize that no matter what your job is, no matter what it is you do in it, no matter who your boss is or even your boss's boss, what you do in your job is actually done in service to King Jesus! He is the One who deployed you there for this time of your life, and it is for him that you ultimately work.

YOU WORK FOR THE KING, AND THAT CHANGES ... EVERYTHING!

That's really the big idea of this book. No matter what you do, your job has inherent purpose and meaning because you are doing it ultimately for the King. *Who you work for is more important than what you do.* The world will tell you otherwise. The world will tell you that life finds its meaning in success at work, or that work is just a necessary evil on the path to leisure. All those ways of thinking are lies. You *do* work for someone beyond your boss. You work for Jesus. That fact is the most important thing you can know and remember about your work. It's much more important than the job itself, regardless of whether you're a homemaker, a banker, a political staffer, a construction worker, a barista, or a corporate executive. No matter what you are doing, you are doing it to glorify Jesus.

If you keep that one big idea in mind, it will change the way you think about your work and engage in your work. Why? Because when glorifying Jesus is our primary motivation, our work—regardless of what that work is in its particulars—becomes an act of worship. We are freed completely from thinking that our work is without meaning and purpose, and we are equally freed from thinking our work holds some *ultimate* meaning. Even more, we discover anew the connection between our jobs and our primary identity as disciples of Jesus. We stop disengaging from our role as disciples from nine to five each day. On the contrary, our engagement with our jobs becomes one of the primary ways we express our discipleship to and love for our Lord.

Work matters. Nobody disputes that. But working *for the King* matters more. As we'll see throughout this book, this realization provides both the day-to-day motivation for our work *and* practical answers to some difficult situations we encounter in the workplace. More than that, it puts work in its rightful place—full of meaning and purpose, but not in competition with the One for whom the work is done in the first place. We work, and that matters. But it matters above all because it's done for King Jesus.

IDLENESS AND IDOLATRY: THE WRONG WAYS TO THINK ABOUT WORK

Remembering that we work for the King and doing our jobs every day in light of that reality aren't easy. It's far easier to slip into thinking wrongly about our jobs than to do the hard work of keeping a godly perspective on them. And there are so many ways to get it wrong, aren't there? We find ourselves grumbling about our jobs or being lazy in them. We do just enough to keep ourselves out of trouble. Or, on the other hand, we find ourselves giving our lives over to our jobs and neglecting our families, our churches, and even our own spiritual health. It all seems so complicated.

But is it really? When we get right down to it, it seems that most of the sins we face when it comes to our jobs can be boiled down to a couple of pitfalls. On the one hand, we can let our job become an *idol*. Our work can become the primary object of our passions, our energy, and our love. We end up worshiping our job. On the other hand, we can slip into being *idle* in our work. When we fail to see God's purposes in our work, we don't really care much about it. We fail to give any attention to it, or we despise it and generally neglect our responsibility to serve as if we are serving the Lord. Unfortunately, idleness *in* work and idolatry *of* work are both celebrated in our society. We tend to praise those who make work the center of their lives, as well as those who have somehow pushed it out of their lives entirely. Both of these pitfalls, though — idleness and idolatry — are deadly misunderstandings of how God wants us to think about our jobs.

We'll explore both idolatry and idleness in more detail later. For now, it's enough to recognize that neither of them square well with the biblical idea that we work for King Jesus. How can we be idle — working without purpose and meaning — if the King himself has assigned our work to us and if we do it in service to him? How can we be content slacking off in our jobs and doing them halfheartedly if, in reality, we do what we do *for him*? When we work for the King, idleness in our work is simply not an option. But neither is idolatry. If our work is a means of rendering service to the King and worshiping him, we must fight the temptation to make our work the center of our lives. Jesus, not our job, deserves to be the central object of our heart's devotion.

A LOOK AHEAD

The two of us have served in both the marketplace and in ministry. Sebastian (Seb) has been an employee, a boss, an owner, and an entrepreneur, as well as a husband, father, church member, and lay leader in his church. Greg has done many of those things as well, and he also serves as pastor of a church. Together, we have wrestled with the questions we have raised, and we've turned to God's Word to better understand what it means for Christians to be faithful workers, serving King Jesus in a secular world. We are simply a businessman and a pastor who have reflected on these questions and hope to share some useful thoughts with you. We wrote this book because *we* need to be reminded regularly how to apply the gospel to our work.

This book is not a theology of work. It is not intended to lay out everything the Bible teaches about work or to answer every question Christians may have about work. There are some thorny theological issues we won't acknowledge or address. We hope you're not disappointed. Our hope is that this book will help some Christians to see a little more clearly why God has given them work to do and how they might be thinking about work in sinful ways. We hope this book will help some Christians forsake both idolatry and idleness in favor of a more biblical way of thinking about work as service to King Jesus.

In the first four chapters of the book, we'll take a close look at both idolatry of work and idleness in work and then consider how a biblical understanding that we work for Jesus challenges and disarms both those sins. In chapters 5 – 11, we'll try to apply this biblical mind-set to a number of practical questions. One final note: we intend for this book in its entirety to be "spoken" by both of us. Occasionally, however, you'll run across a story that's written using "I" instead of "we." When that happens, we'll try to indicate which of us is telling the story.

We don't know why you picked up this book. Maybe as you've read this introduction, you've already admitted to yourself, "Yep, I have idolized my work," or "That's me. I've fallen into idleness in my work. I just don't see God's point in it all." Maybe you're a new Christian, and you're wondering how this new life you have in Jesus works itself out in your nine to five. Or maybe it's something else entirely. Our hope is that no matter what confusion you've harbored about what it means to work as a Christian in a godless world, the big idea we've talked about will begin to free you to experience purpose and meaning in your work. If your tendency is toward idleness — toward a false idea that God doesn't care about your work — then we hope this book will remind you that you work for King Jesus and that your work matters very much. On the other hand, if your tendency is toward idolatry — toward a false idea that work matters above all and holds the key to ultimate satisfaction — then we pray this book will transform your work from an object of worship into a means of worshiping the one true God.

More than anything, we hope you will be encouraged to grow in your love for and knowledge of the Lord Jesus Christ as you pursue his purposes for you in the workplace.

Note: If you are reading this book with others—

At the end of each chapter we provide several questions and Scripture passages for you to study that will help you to further reflect on and think about the ideas in that chapter. These questions are designed to be used as you read the book with a friend or a small group. Consider who can walk through these with you. It's important to have other people you can be honest with and who can be honest with you. Proverbs 16:13 reads, "Kings take pleasure in honest lips; they value the one who speaks what is right," and Proverbs 27:6 states, "Wounds from a friend can be trusted." Find people who can speak the truth and wound you in love.

CHAPTER 1

THE IDOLATRY *OF* WORK

I (Seb) remember the first time I realized that work had become an idol for me. The moment came just after a high point in my professional career path. A friend and I had started a company, and for the last few years we had poured ourselves—heart, soul, and body—into it, and the company had done well. Five years into the venture, for all kinds of reasons, we decided the time had come to sell the company. The group to which we ended up selling had pursued us for several years, but our answer had always been, "No thanks." This time, however, the time seemed right. Over the next few months, we went through a surreal experience of negotiating the sale. When the last phase—the "Lawyers Talking to Accountants" phase—was done, it was time to close the deal.

I still remember the closing. I was in Anaheim, California, when my business partner called from Washington, DC, to give me the play-by-play of the signing. He read through the documents once more. I asked a few questions about some details, and then he signed and faxed off the papers. The ownership of our company was transferred to someone else, and a not-insignificant chunk of change to us.

It was a great day! It was also the beginning of a new era in my life. God was about to teach me something new about myself and about the way I approached my work. Once the dust had settled from the sale, I was faced with a new reality: I had to find something else to do. Eager, optimistic, and excited to see where God would lead me in my professional life, I started looking around for fresh opportunities.

I looked for a long time. A really long time. Doors closed. Applications were rejected. Phone calls were ignored. E-mails were "lost." At the end of several months of searching, I was running out of ideas. I trusted that God was leading me somewhere, but it was to a place I had never anticipated or desired. He had led me to unemployment, and right along with it to hopelessness and a profound and utterly unfamiliar sense of self-doubt. My emotions had plummeted from the top of the world to a place of despair in just a few months. My hopes, which had been so high during the sale of my company, were now ruined. My faith in God was barely limping along.

How did this happen? Why did I experience such a profound shift of my emotions and hopes? Why was my faith shaken so deeply? Looking back, I can see why. My hopes had not been rooted in God; they had been rooted in my circumstances — in my professional success and in my ability to control the future. Work had become an idol to me. My sense of well-being — my very identity as a person — was wrapped up in my professional success. Once that was gone, I was devastated. My god had been ripped out from under me. And I fell hard.

WHAT IS AN IDOL?

What does it mean when we say that a person has made work an idol? Does it simply mean he or she works too hard? Is it idolatrous to enjoy what we do, to find pleasure in our work? How about enjoying what we do *a lot?* Is it wrong to want to leave our mark on the world, to "put a dent in the universe" (as Steve Jobs once put it)? These can all be perfectly good motivations for our work, and none of them is necessarily wrong. The trouble starts when our pursuit of enjoyment or influence or status in our work begins to make our work the source of ultimate satisfaction or meaning for us. When that happens, our work has become our god.

The Bible tells us that our hearts are desperately prone to worshiping idols. We are worshipers by our very nature as human beings. We *will* find something to bow before, something to give our lives and our devotion to. We *will* worship something. We *will* center our lives around something.

Our compulsion to worship is not a bad thing! God made us for worship. Worship is a very good thing as long as the object of our worship is *worthy* of our worship. So what is the right object for our worship? Only God himself. Jesus once said, "Worship the Lord your God and serve him *only*" (Luke 4:8, emphasis added). Our worship should be reserved for God. He alone should command our highest devotion, and it should be around him that we center and organize our lives. When that pride of place goes to anything or anyone else, we have bowed our knees to an idol.

In the Old Testament, idols were just like you'd picture them — the little golden statues that Indiana Jones swiped from the Temple of Doom. Of course, they weren't always golden, and they weren't always small. People worshiped these physical objects because they believed they somehow represented real gods, spiritual beings with power to meet their needs. People performed all kinds of worshipful acts toward their idols, casting riches at their feet, clothing them in the finest clothes, even physically bowing down to them. They organized their lives around their devotion to the gods these idols represented.

We tend not to be quite so crass in our idolatry today. Typically, we don't have little golden statues to venerate, nor do we gather at temples to lavish gifts on those statues. We've become more sophisticated in our idolatry, but our tendency to worship things other than God is just as strong as ever. For many people today, their passion is their job and all of the things their job can provide for them — money, status, identity, pleasure, and purpose. Our jobs capture our hearts and our devotion. We give ourselves to them day in and day out. They become the primary object of our passions, our energy, and our love. We may not be willing to admit it, but we worship our jobs.

Luke 18:18–29 helps us better understand what it means to let something become an idol for us. A rich ruler comes to Jesus to learn what is required of him to inherit eternal life. Jesus tells him, and the man excitedly says that this is exactly what his life has *always* looked like! But then Jesus probes the one area of his life that the young man wants to keep for himself. "You still lack one thing," Jesus says. "Sell everything you have and give to the poor, and you will have treasure in heaven. Then come, follow me." The Bible says that when the young man heard this "he became very sad, because he was very wealthy." Jesus thus revealed the man's idol — his love for money and the security and status it provided to him. His idol kept him from following Jesus.

Do you see the point of this story? It gives us one of the clearest and simplest pictures of idolatry in the entire Bible. *An idol is something that you desire more than you desire Jesus.*

DO YOU MAKE AN IDOL OF YOUR WORK?

It's easy to make your job an idol. Our culture drives us to be successful, but success is typically defined in specific ways. Think about the conversations you have when you meet someone new. One of the first questions you likely ask is, "What do you do?" At this point, the pressure is on to convince the other person that what we do is important and that we are good at it. The social cues around us push us to find our identity in our jobs—in the things we do.

Idolizing your work, however, is more than just a bad idea; it's a deadly spiritual danger. If your pursuit of joy, satisfaction, and meaning centers on "what you do" and "what you are accomplishing," you'll find nothing but emptiness at the end of that road. Deep and lasting satisfaction can only be found when our worship is directed at the one who alone deserves it—Jesus Christ.

Our jobs become idols when we overidentify with them. Our work becomes the primary consumer of our time, our attention, and our passions, as well as the primary means for measuring our happiness and our dissatisfaction in life. So what are some of the warning signs that this is happening? Here are some of the most common ways we idolize our jobs. See if any of these describe you.

1. Your work is the primary source of your satisfaction.

It is all too easy to look for fulfillment from your work, finding your ultimate purpose in job performance and success in the workplace. For some, this kind of idolatry takes the subtle form of insisting they will do only what they were "made to do" and refusing to do—or do well—anything less than what they are passionate about. For others, this can take the form of a constant, grinding frustration—a sense that their work is not completely fulfilling. For others, it's the opposite—a deep-seated self-satisfaction in what they have already accomplished.

What about you? Does success at work fill a big need in your life? Do you find your mood radically shifting as your professional stock goes up and down? Our jobs can never provide the kind of satisfaction and fulfillment we're demanding of them. They simply were not intended to bear these expectations. So it shouldn't surprise us when the satisfaction we experience through our work fades or fails to sustain us.

It's like a child riding his scooter. He can ride it around the driveway well enough, but then he gets angry when the scooter doesn't fly. We may find it humorous or amusing, but the little boy grows increasingly frustrated and angry, kicking the scooter and shouting at it. Of course, the problem is simple: scooters aren't designed to fly. The child is confused about the purpose of the scooter—it's not *supposed* to fly! It's meant to be ridden. If the child had appropriate expectations for his scooter, he'd enjoy it more.

The same is true of our jobs. If we have appropriate expectations for our jobs, we will likely find ourselves enjoying them more. Our jobs were never intended to carry the weight of providing us with ultimate, lasting satisfaction. And when we try to make them carry that freight, we will find ourselves quickly disappointed.

2. Your work is all about being the best so you can make a name for yourself. Your job can become an idol when you place an undue emphasis on the pursuit of excellence. Of course, there's nothing inherently wrong with working hard and doing your work well. In fact, that's something God requires of us! The problem is in our desire to be *recognized* as being good at something. This can easily become an idol. We want to look good. We want people to take notice of us and praise us for our abilities. We want them to value us and ultimately ... to glorify us.

This expression of workplace idolatry often leads to a perpetually competitive mind-set. Mentally, we're always keeping score. "Am I as good as those guys?" "How do my accomplishments stack up against that person?" Some competition can be healthy, driving us to reach a little further and work a little harder. However, this becomes disastrous when our desire to be at the top begins to rule our hearts. Even when we succeed, the idolatry of success can leave us feeling like it's just not good enough—an unrelenting perfectionism. And if we don't succeed, the idolatry of success can lead to soul-destroying discouragement or grim resignation.

3. Your work becomes primarily about making a difference in the world. Another way our work becomes an idol is when we think that the ultimate purpose of our work is to bring some benefit to the people around us. There is something profoundly *right* about a desire to make a difference in the world around us. However, that desire can also elevate itself into idolatry if we believe that the value of our work is ultimately determined by its impact on the world.

When our desire to have an impact takes priority, it is possible that God and his purposes will be squeezed out of the picture. This expression of idolatry fills us with pride, as we take credit for the things our work is accomplishing instead of recognizing these achievements as gifts from God. Making a difference or working to "change the world" can also lead us to neglect other God-given responsibilities. We justify our neglect because we are doing something good—serving others. Then if our efforts don't produce the results we want to see, we get discouraged and angry; we become frustrated and think our work was simply a waste of time.

Every form of idolatry—every act of worshiping something that is not worthy of our worship—will bear bitter fruit in our lives. Good and godly desires can quickly be transformed into idols, producing covetousness, comparison, dissatisfaction, and unrelenting competitiveness. Idolatry is the classic bait and switch. Idols promise fulfillment, but they never provide it. We are left with increasing dissatisfaction and unfulfilled longing.

WHY WORK IS A TERRIBLE GOD

God tells us that nothing in this world is worthy of our worship except Jesus. Everything else, including our jobs, will fail to satisfy in this life and will be useless for the next one.

Why is that? Why can't we find deep and lasting satisfaction in our jobs? Why don't they bring about the fulfillment we so often convince ourselves they will? The answer is that our hearts will *always* grasp for more. If you give yourself to the idol of work, you'll find it is an impossible taskmaster, a slave driver that can never be completely satisfied. It will always disappoint us and let us down. It will never finally grant the satisfaction it promises.

I remember the first time I (Seb) recognized this truth. As a freshman at Princeton University, I was walking across campus one day and realized I'd achieved the one driving goal of all the work I'd done throughout high school: I was a student at an Ivy League school! In that same moment, though, I also realized I wasn't satisfied. Why not? Because I realized high school had simply been a stepping-stone to Princeton, and now Princeton had become a stepping-stone to some other goal. Princeton had seemed like the goal, but it really wasn't. I still wasn't satisfied. I wanted more.

Thinking about all this, I started asking myself a simple question: *What's next?*

- So here I am at the fancy college; great, what's next?
- A great job right out of college; check, what's next?

The logic of idolatry is clear in my thinking. There will *always* be a next step, *always* something more for me to attain. Working for myself and my own fulfillment will *always* end in dissatisfaction.

- Started and successfully built a great company; all right, what's next?
- Huge home and vacation house; got 'em, what's next?
- Produced a Hollywood movie; what's next?

- Bought a baseball team and can treat it like my fantasy team; yea, what's next?
- Richer than Bill Gates—$40 billion in the bank and $40 billion given to charities; what's next?

The problem became astonishingly clear: at every step along the way I was looking forward to the next thing, something that might finally fulfill that promise of satisfaction for me. But I couldn't find it.

It's not just the fact that our hearts will always grasp for "What's next?" though; it's also the bracing fact that the Bible tells us our work is cursed! When human beings rebelled against God and plunged the world into sin, our labor became back-breakingly difficult, and its fruits hard-won and fleeting. We only make matters worse when we fail to recognize that reality and start seeking ultimate, lasting satisfaction in our work.

Here's the fundamental problem with letting our work become an idol: There is always more that can be done, more that can be achieved. There is always a "What's next?" to pursue. We can always improve our work just a little more. We can always help more people, make the city a little bit better. We can always make our work a little more efficient and a little easier. The goalposts keep moving, and satisfaction proves elusive.

SO WHAT'S THE FIX FOR IDOLATRY OF WORK?

The bottom line truth of all this is that this world is simply not worth living for. Oh, it claims to be! And it makes all kinds of promises about the good it can give us if we just burn our lives out in its service. But only God himself is truly worth living for. Only he can bring ultimate, lasting satisfaction.

So what about you? How have you been looking too much for happiness, joy, fulfillment, or purpose in your job? Have you found yourself wanting the good your job promises more than you've desired Jesus? Have you made your work an idol? If so, the solution is simple, though not easy: You need to repent! You need to turn from that futile and wrong way of thinking, recognize your idolatry of work for what it is, and refocus your mind on *working as an act of worship to God*. When you do that, you'll find to your great joy that the goalposts suddenly stop moving. That's because once you ground your life and joy and satisfaction in God, there is no "What's next?"

Why not? Because there is no need for anything more.

1. Read and Reflect: Luke 18:18–29

2. Is devotion to your work a primary organizing principle of your life? What would those who know you best (friends, family members) say?

3. The chapter lists several warnings about ways we can sinfully make work an idol. In what ways do you make work an idol?

4. Making work an idol can be a subtle sin, one often cloaked in otherwise seemingly good intentions, like working hard, earning money, and so forth. Name some practical ways you can guard against making work an idol.

5. Think of a time in your life when you were satisfied with an accomplishment in your work. Maybe it was a well-written paper, a well-delivered presentation, or a completed building project. How long did that sense of accomplishment last? What does that experience suggest about the futility of making your work an idol?

6. What are the "What's Nexts?" in your life? How can you hold these loosely?

CHAPTER 2

IDLENESS *IN* WORK

I (Seb) started my first business in high school. A family friend asked me one day if I'd be interested in getting paid to seal his deck. I went to the hardware store and got lessons on how to use all the tools necessary to do the job: power washers, stains, seals, techniques—the whole nine yards. I did the job for him, and as I was working, inspiration hit. Rather than just enjoy the spoils of one afternoon's work, I decided to print up flyers and plaster the neighborhood with them. "Professional Deck Sealing!" Within a day I'd secured two more jobs. My fledgling start-up was off the ground.

My driving goal in this business was not to provide superior service or even to beautify the neighborhood, much less to glorify God through a job well done. My goal was to seal as many decks as possible, in as little time as possible, for as much money as possible, and with as little effort as possible! The end of this story is not good. My maniacal focus on speed, cost, and ease made for some pretty shoddy work. I didn't think it was necessary to move potted plants, for instance, before sealing the decks. So a few of my customers discovered unsealed circles on their decks when they moved their pots in the fall. I chose not to protect the sides of the house either, and so I ended up leaving a shiny streak at the base of the brick. To my embarrassment, more than one customer had to ask me to redo the job — and warned me to clean up my filthy mess when I was done!

Of course, at the most basic level, this was just bad business practice. Because I was doing such a terrible job, my business was inevitably going to suffer. Yet as inadvisable as such shoddiness on the job may be from a purely business perspective, the more important issue was my heart. I believed that mediocre work was OK. The quality of my work didn't really mean anything to me. It was simply a means to an end — a way to get money and serve my own selfish needs and desires.

As we saw in the previous chapter, we can overidentify with our work and make it into an idol. But the opposite is also true for many of us — we *under*identify with our work. We care too *little* about it and find ourselves being idle in our work. Idleness literally means *not working*, just sitting idly by while others provide for us. We all know that's bad, so we'll assume the average person reading this book isn't quite as dramatic in being idle. When we talk about being "idle" in our work, we don't mean just sitting around and doing nothing at all.

So don't think you're off the hook! There are subtle forms of idleness that are harder to spot than simple inactivity. These expressions of idleness have less to do with the productivity of our hands, and everything to do with the motives and desires of our hearts.

WHAT IS IDLENESS?

One of the most subtle — and perhaps most dangerous — forms of idleness in our work is our failure to recognize God's purposes for us in the workplace. We may be active in our work, but we have concluded that our work simply doesn't matter. We may believe that our value as a Christian is restricted to what we do at church, and the work we do is just a necessary evil we endure in order to earn tithe dollars and support the mission of the church. Or we may think that if we're not passionate about the job God has given us, it's not our true calling. It's all right to slack off. "I'll give it my all," we say, "when I'm doing what makes me passionate." Idleness can also take the form of a "slackivism"—measures taken by a person to only do the minimum required to get through the day. Some adopt a "work to live" philosophy, seeing their work as a gross but necessary intrusion into real life. Or you may have a recurring case of the "Monday blues," a sense that your real life comes to an end when it's time to go to work again.

You get the point. Being idle does not necessarily mean inactivity—a lack of productivity. It can be an inactivity of the heart, an inability or unwillingness to see or embrace God's purposes in the work he's given you to do. It's a heart that does not grasp how God is using your work to shape you, a heart that denies your Christian responsibility to serve "as if you were serving the Lord" (Ephesians 6:7). When this kind of thinking takes hold in our minds, the results are devastating. Despondency, joylessness, complaining, discontentedness, laziness, passivity, people pleasing, score settling, corner cutting, Monday-dreading gloom—these are the fruits of being idle in our work.

THE BIBLE ON IDLENESS

Writing to the Thessalonian believers, Paul clearly and unequivocally teaches that the most dramatic form of idleness—inactivity—should never mark Christians. "The one who is unwilling to work," he writes, "shall not eat" (2 Thessalonians 3:10). That's a bracing truth, and a good reminder for all of us.

But as we've suggested, the Bible warns us against more than simply "doing nothing." It also warns us against the sin of simply "doing something"! One of the most useful passages for thinking about this (and one we'll return to again and again in this book) is Colossians 3:22–24:

> Slaves, obey your earthly masters in everything; and do it, not only when their eye is on you and to curry their favor, but with sincerity of heart and reverence for the Lord. Whatever you do, work at it with all your heart, as working for the Lord, not for human masters, since you know that you will receive an inheritance from the Lord as a reward. It is the Lord Christ you are serving.

Do you see what Paul is saying here? He begins with a warning against doing nothing. If you are a slave, then obey your masters in everything. *Just do it,* he tells them. But he goes one step further. "Just doing it" isn't enough either. As slaves, they should work and serve "with sincerity of heart and reverence for the Lord." They are to do their work with all their heart, "as working for the Lord, not for human masters," and they are to do it with a recognition that it is ultimately the Lord Jesus Christ they are serving!

We'll say a bit more about the whole idea of slavery in the Bible a bit later, but for now, we need to see that Paul is making a full frontal assault here on a mind-set of idleness in our work. And he doesn't just target inactivity. He points out that those who work for others should not just avoid doing *nothing*; they should do *everything* they do with a heart full of understanding that God cares deeply about everything we do, that we do our work as an act of worship to him, and that the service we render is ultimately to him and not to any person. Paul wants Christians to see that their work matters, that it is actually a high-profile arena in which God glorifies himself and at the same time makes us more like Jesus.

ARE YOU IDLE IN YOUR WORK?

How do you know when you've allowed yourself to become idle in your work? What are the warning signs that you're not grasping God's purposes for your life in your job? Here are some common ways in which people let idle thinking creep into their work. See if any of these describe you.

1. Your work is merely a means to an end, a place to serve your own needs. Sometimes this kind of thinking can be pretty blatant and obvious. I work, some people say, so I can play. I'm in it for the money and the things money can buy. Or it can take on a veneer of spirituality. "I work," you might say, "so I can be free to serve my church, and so I can give money to my church." Either way, it's pretty clear that a person who thinks like this doesn't care much about their job at all. They only care about the other things their job allows them to do.

What's wrong with this line of thinking? It ignores the fact that God has purposes for us *in our work itself.* Our jobs are more than just a means to an end—whether that end is selfish enjoyment or service in the church. Our work is more than something we "slog through." However menial, however boring, however unmatched to our interests, our jobs are one of the key ways in which God matures us as Christians and brings glory to himself. God has a purpose for our work.

2. Your work totally frustrates you. Work will always carry with it some level of frustration; that's why it's not worthy of our worship. Yet sometimes we go too far with our frustrations and grow blind to God's aims for us in our work. We let our frustration control us and infect our hearts with bitterness and anger. For those who recognize that satisfaction and purpose come as gifts from God, the frustration we experience at work shouldn't lead to discouragement. It should simply remind us that our work is not ultimate, that we shouldn't make an idol of our work or look to it for ultimate satisfaction. Our frustration turns our eyes back to God, increasing our dependency on him, and reminding us that our responsibility is to do our work in service and as an act of worship to him.

3. Your work becomes divorced from your Christian discipleship. More than a few Christians think of their work as something they have to do from nine to five, Monday through Friday, so they can do the real work of being a Christian in the evenings and on weekends. If this describes you, read Colossians 3 again. Our work is not something we do in addition to our growth as a follower of Christ. Our work, here and now, is an expression of our Christian faith. Everything we do is an act of worship to God and an act of following Jesus, whether it is at home, at work, or at church. When you prepare a Sunday school lesson, you are serving God and following Jesus. When you attend a leadership team meeting at church, you are serving God and following Jesus. When you lead your small group or participate in a service project, you are serving God and following Jesus. That's all true! But it's also true that when you're writing a memo for your boss, you're worshiping God and following Jesus. When you're talking on the phone to a customer, you're worshiping God and following Jesus. When you're placing an order or driving a rivet, you're worshiping God and following Jesus. It's all worship, and it's all discipleship. "Whatever you do," Paul writes, "work at it with all your heart." Why? Because you work for the King. Because it is the Lord Christ you are serving.

WHY IDLENESS IS NOT AN OPTION
Look at this guy:

Obviously, someone was having a little fun with Photoshop here. But think about this picture for just a second. If you saw this guy walking down the street, I doubt your first thought would be, "Wow, that dude is in really great shape." It probably wouldn't even be, "Wow, I'm really impressed by your right side. Good work!" No, your reaction would be more like, "Yikes! Something went wrong there!"

Yet we make the same mistake when we allow ourselves to think of our work as merely a means to an end. When we ignore God's purposes in our work and think of it as "just a job" we have to "slog through" in order to get to the important stuff, we're pulling the spiritual equivalent of knocking out a quick set of five curls on our left arm so we can get to the really important task of working out our right arm! We end up with a terrible imbalance in our spiritual life — robust discipleship with our family and church, but a weak and emaciated discipleship in our work life.

Christians can't be content with this kind of spiritual imbalance. As we have seen, the Bible calls us to be disciples of Jesus and worshipers of God in every area of our lives. In everything we do, we should work as those who are working for Jesus. Don't fool yourself into thinking that God doesn't care about your work.

Believing that God doesn't care about our work can lead us into disobedience and sin. Christians often find themselves doing things at work that they'd never do anywhere else — treating people with contempt, losing their tempers, stealing time or supplies, cutting corners or fudging what's right and wrong. When we decide that our jobs don't really matter to God, we're less careful to keep God at the front of our minds when we're dealing with others. We no longer think to ask ourselves, "What would please God in this particular situation and circumstance?" We find ourselves, without even realizing it, doing our work without thinking about Jesus at all.

How would your work change if you began to approach your job as an arena for God's glory and your own growth and discipleship? It changes everything. Your interactions with customers and bosses and employees become opportunities to show God's love and goodness to them. That memo you have to write now becomes an opportunity to serve in the name of the King. Every situation that might normally drive you to irritation and frustration — missed deadlines, tension in relationships with coworkers — now becomes an opportunity for you to pause, pray, and think, "OK, so God has brought this situation into my life. What does he want me to learn from it? What have I learned that he wants me to apply to this situation? How is this going to strengthen my faith and bring him glory?" Asking these questions — and then acting in light of them — is precisely what it means to fight idleness in work and "serve wholeheartedly, as if you were serving the Lord" (Ephesians 6:7).

WHAT'S THE FIX FOR IDLENESS IN WORK?

Here's the bottom line: our jobs matter to God. He created us to work, and even though Adam's sin has ensured that our work will be shot through with frustration, God still plans to use our jobs to bring himself glory and to do good in and through our lives. This means it is not an option for us to be idle in our jobs. If you are guilty of idleness in your work, again, the solution is for you to repent — to turn from wrong ways of thinking, recognize your idleness in work for what it is (sin), and recommit yourself to God's purposes for your job.

1. Read and Reflect: 2 Thessalonians 3:6 – 15; Colossians 3:22 – 24

2. Think about your current job. Are you more prone to being idle or making your work an idol?

3. How would the way you approach your work change if you truly believed each day that God had his purposes for you in your work?

4. Idleness can be a sinful response to our experiences of futility and frustration in our work. Think of a time you responded to this feeling by being lazy or resentful in your work. What can you specifically do differently next time to honor God?

5. From what we know, Jesus was likely a carpenter, Peter was a fisherman, and Paul was a tentmaker. Each was familiar with the toil of manual work. It is hard to imagine them being lazy in their woodworking, or fishing, or tentmaking. How can you think, speak, and care too little about the simple responsibilities God has given you?

6. Genesis teaches that God is a worker. He created, ordered, and designed. List four or five implications for your life based on this truth.

CHAPTER 3

THE GOSPEL
IN THE WORKPLACE

We've seen we shouldn't make an idol *of* work, and we shouldn't let ourselves become idle *in* our work. So how *should* we think about our jobs? How do our jobs fit into the rest of our lives as followers of Christ? How does our Christian faith color and affect the way we do our work and the way we think about our work? In a world in which most people think of their jobs as either a necessary evil or as the source of their identity and fulfillment, what is it that uniquely brings meaning and purpose to our jobs as Christians?

Begin by asking yourself these questions: What difference does it make in my workplace that I am a Christian? Does it make me a more moral person? Do I have integrity? Am I less competitive than others? Do I always have a smile on my face? Is it that I'll go the extra mile for a coworker and stay late to help on a project?

This is all great! But is that all there is to it? Does our Christian faith only work itself out in our jobs in these ways? Or is there more to being a Christian who works? Being a Christian means your life has been changed and transformed by the gospel of Jesus Christ. God loved you and sent his Son Jesus to stand as your substitute, living and dying on the cross in your place for your sin. He rose again, breaking the power of death, and by repenting and trusting in him, you have been saved. Being a Christian in the workplace means the truth of the gospel should work itself out in every detail of your life, including your job. As Christians, we want to see the entire world in light of the gospel. We want to experience how the amazing truth of this good news brightens and illuminates everything — even the fluorescent-lit corners of our nine-to-five jobs!

We hope the previous two chapters have helped you begin to evaluate your heart and examine more carefully your motivations for working. We've asked you to think about whether you are more prone to make an idol of your work or to be idle in it. We've asked you to consider why both of these approaches to work are nothing short of disastrous. Of course, every one of us is guilty of falling into these traps from time to time, and sometimes we fall into both of them — even at the same time! So it's not enough to diagnose the problem. We also have to spend time thinking about the specific ways in which the good news of Jesus confronts and defeats the idolatry and idleness in our hearts.

JESUS' WORK CHANGES EVERYTHING — INCLUDING OUR OWN WORK

The key to confronting and defeating idolatry and idleness is understanding how the gospel of Jesus cuts the root of both of these lies. The Bible tells us we are sinners. We are rebels against God and are "slaves to sin." In fact, the Bible teaches us we are sinners who owe a massive debt to God, yet instead of paying off that debt, we continue working overtime against him! Instead of working ourselves out of debt, our wages actually plunge us more deeply into it. The gospel is good news to slaves bound in sin who owe a debt they can never repay. The good news is that God sent his Son, Jesus Christ, to take on himself the debt we owe to God. Standing as our substitute, in our place, Jesus lived the life we failed to live and died the death we deserved to die. He rose again from the dead, victorious over death, sin, and the grave.

How does the work that Jesus has done change our lives? The gospel is the announcement that God is ready and willing to count our sin against Jesus and graciously give us the right status, identity, and position of his Son, Jesus. By turning away from our sins and relying on Jesus to save us, we become united to him. Our debt is paid in full by his death in our place, and all the rewards he won through his own life of obedience are graciously and lovingly given to us!

You may be reading this book right now and may not be a Christian. If this is true, you should take some time to think about what we've just stated in those last two paragraphs. No kidding—it's the most important message you'll ever hear! Ask a Christian friend to explain more of this to you, or pick up another book that will explain the good news of Jesus in more detail (we know one or two we can recommend!). You can't simply ignore it. The gospel of Jesus is life-changing truth.

If you are a Christian, we want to challenge you to begin connecting the reality of what God has done for you in Christ to your job, thinking carefully about how this applies to and changes the way you think about your work. Do you see how the gospel severs the root of idolatry *and* idleness, replacing our motives for working in these ways?

Let's first consider idolatry. Jesus' work for us, in our place and on our behalf, has really and truly secured salvation from our sin and eternal life for us—the only life that can provide deep and lasting satisfaction for our souls. What's more, God offers this gift to us without cost! It's not something we can earn or work to achieve. This means our jobs can never give us what we truly want. Only Jesus can. By his life, death, and resurrection, he has already achieved for us the highest joy, the highest meaning, the highest significance, and the highest prize. When we believe our jobs can provide this for us, we forget the gospel and believe a lie.

The truth of the gospel cuts the root of idleness as well. If it's true that our lives now belong to Jesus, then everything in our lives has new significance—including our jobs. We are not free to "mail it in" on anything! The Dutch theologian Abraham Kuyper declared, "There is not one square inch of the entire creation about which Jesus Christ does not cry out, 'This is mine! This belongs to me!'" That's true, and it includes our lives and our jobs as well, for there is also not one spare minute Jesus does not claim as his. This means idleness is not an option for those who believe the gospel.

These are the big-picture truths, but it's worth unpacking this in more detail. Once we become Christians and begin to work for Jesus, everything changes. How, exactly, does the gospel change our perspective on work?

You Work for a New Master

If you trust in Jesus Christ's life and death in your place—if you have given your life to him in faith—then you work for a new master in everything you do. Where you once were a slave to sin, you are now a slave to righteousness (Romans 6:17–18). Where once you were an enemy of God, you are now a child of God and co-heir with Christ (Romans 8:16–17; Galatians 3:26–29). Where once you pursued the passions of the flesh and the praise of other people, you now work for the King. It is Jesus Christ whom you serve.

You Have a New Assignment

Odds are your job puts a bewildering array of obligations and assignments on you. Some are put on you by your boss, others by your coworkers, still others by yourself. There are clients to answer, calls to make, trips to take, orders to place, projects to finish, accounts to close, lunches to eat, and a thousand little tasks in between. How do you make sense of it all? Is there anything that organizes it all and keeps it all in perspective?

The answer is yes. If you are a follower of Christ, you look to Jesus to reorder your assignments and obligations, and he is very clear about what matters most. In Matthew 22, someone asked Jesus which of the bewildering array of commandments was most important. His answer is wonderfully unambiguous: " 'Love the Lord your God with all your heart and with all your soul and with all your mind.' This is the first and greatest commandment. And the second is like it: 'Love your neighbor as yourself' " (Matthew 22:37 – 39).

When you become a Christian, your overarching, overriding, life-driving assignment becomes as clear as crystal: You are to love God and love others. That assignment trumps everything else. No matter what you do for a living, you are working for something different than what the non-Christians around you are working for. Yes, money is important. Yes, advancement in your career can be good. Yes, you want to help your boss and do a good job. But ultimately you are in your job so you learn to love God and other people better. This is your new assignment.

You Have a New Confidence

So many of the problems we confront in the workplace boil down to issues of self-worth and confidence. I slave away at my job, desperate to move past my peers, because that's how I'll know I'm OK — a person who has value. I become extremely sensitive to criticism and completely deflated when I get negative feedback, because my self-worth is entirely wrapped up in my job.

It's important to notice what we aren't saying here. We aren't saying that the gospel gives you a new *self-worth*. Instead, it gives you a new *confidence*. The point of the gospel isn't how great *you* are; it's how great *Jesus* is, and how deeply you benefit from *his* greatness. Knowing you are loved by God in spite of yourself turns out to be the real answer to all the things you think you need self-esteem to achieve. You may think you need self-esteem (feeling like you are a person of worth and value) to feel acceptable. But the truth is that you are accepted, not because you are a person of worth and value, but because of what Jesus has done for you as a lost sinner. *You* think you need self-esteem, and *the world* thinks you need to think more highly of yourself. But what you really need is to understand that everything you thought self-esteem could provide is really found in Christ and his love for you. As a Christian, you don't need to esteem yourself more highly. You have a new confidence knowing that Christ loves you—and that changes everything.

You Have New Rewards

What are you working for? Money, power, fame, and comfort? A school building named after you? A company that lives on after you're gone? A house at the beach? Helping a lot of people? Using your talents? The rewards Jesus provides are far greater than anything the world offers. And they last forever!

Consider what Paul writes to the slaves in Colossians 3. Why does he tell them to work with sincerity of heart, as working for the Lord and not for human masters? Because they know that they "will receive an inheritance from the Lord as a reward" (Colossians 3:24)! If that is true (and it is), then no vacation house can compete with this reward. There's no greater reward in the universe than what Jesus gives to those who work for him.

Once you accept this truth and believe it, it begins to change the way you approach your work. No longer do you look to your job to provide you with ultimate rewards, because you know that the greatest rewards you can ever have are secure for you in Jesus. You are free, not to make your work into an idol, but to make it an arena for loving God and loving others. You're free from the trap of idleness, from growing frustrated and bitter in the difficulties or drudgery your job brings. Your happiness is secured elsewhere; you don't have to be discouraged that your job isn't providing it. Instead, you can approach your job—even if you don't like it—as an opportunity to love God more and bring him glory.

Knowing that you work for King Jesus and not for other people changes the way you approach your job. You have a new master, a new assignment, a new confidence, and new rewards— all because of Jesus. That's not just a series of bullet points to pull out of your mental wallet here and there. It's a whole new way of thinking.

And this new way of thinking leads to a newfound freedom in the workplace.

EXPERIENCING FREEDOM IN YOUR DAY-TO-DAY WORK

Having this eternal perspective about your work frees you from both idolatry and idleness in your work. It frees you from thinking that work can provide everything you want. And it frees you from thinking that your job doesn't matter to God.

What does this freedom look like in your day-to-day work? It means you can respond to circumstances and situations differently because your ultimate identity and reward have already been secured by Jesus. That is an awesome anchor for your soul. Without it, it's inevitable that you'll be blown around like a leaf by the winds of stock market gyrations, temporary successes and failures, performance reports, bosses who do or don't treat you well, and your own desires, whether they are met or not. When you are secure in your new identity in Christ, and when you embrace your new assignment from him, you are free to stand firm amid all the nauseating ups and downs of life at work. You have anchored your soul to something that is truly immovable. And it's why who you work for is more important than what you do.

Let's take a look at some of the ways that your identity as a person saved and loved by Jesus gives freedom in the workplace.

1. Working for Jesus gives you freedom to worship God through your work. Worship is our response to who God is and what God has done. When we see God rightly, we want to please him. And one way we do that is in our jobs.

What does worship in the workplace look like? Does it mean singing praise songs quietly to yourself on the job? Well, there's certainly nothing wrong with that! But biblical worship is more than just singing. To worship is to give God the honor he deserves. This means obeying God in every task you perform, knowing that when you do that task with all your heart, you are pleasing God. It means your attitude and aims are no longer tied to yourself and your circumstances. The goal of life is not how much money, power, fame, or comfort you can accrue. Rather, you desire to please God and make much of him.

Even more, worshiping God in the workplace means you find yourself learning about him, seeing his work, and enjoying his presence in your job. When you see creativity, revel in it as a reflection of the Great Creator of the universe! When your boss does a good job leading, rejoice in that as a good gift from God. When your boss doesn't do a good job leading, rejoice that the King of the universe is greater than him! When you see justice prevail, when you help a client get the best price on the best product for their needs, rejoice in those things as a beautiful reflection of God's goodness. When you have an eternal perspective, you are free to worship God in your work.

2. *Working for Jesus gives you freedom to <u>serve others wholeheartedly</u>.* Have you noticed how rare it is to find a truly altruistic person in the workplace? Most people, even the nicest ones, are driven by an agenda. It's incredibly difficult to find someone who simply wants to do good to others. As somebody who is working in order to love God and love others, you can be that person. You *should* be that person! Why? Because all that you really need is already secured for you by Jesus. It's nice to be appreciated by your boss and respected by your peers. But everything you think you need that appreciation and respect for — affirmation, love, acceptance, a sense of well-being, future reward — is already yours in Jesus. You are freed from having your identity tied to what people think about you. You are free to serve them without an agenda.

God has loved you unexpectedly and unashamedly. You can now extend that same love to others. On the job, you can love your coworkers, employees, and bosses by looking out for their good and serving them, not for your own gain or to set yourself up for future success, but simply because you love them. Show them you care about their lives and not just their performance. Buy someone coffee and talk, or offer to forgo your lunch and run an errand for someone. Respond to them graciously, as Christ has been gracious to you. Serve and love your coworkers unexpectedly and unashamedly, because that is how Jesus has served and loved you.

3. *Working for Jesus gives you freedom to trust God in your work.* Work is a source of worry and anxiety. There's no way to escape this. So much can go so wrong in so many different ways. Murphy's law rules the land, and there are days when it seems to be the only law at work in our lives. As someone who works ultimately for the Lord, you have the freedom to trust God instead of giving in to worry. It's not just that Jesus is a great career planner, though. No, we trust him with our future because he has already secured it for eternity. Even if things are going south in our jobs, we have defenses against the crushing power of anxiety. We can work with an open hand and trust God.

Think about a worry you've had at work recently. If you're like us, you probably have several to choose from! Deadlines, feeling overwhelmed by expectations, difficulty with coworkers or your boss—the workplace can be a constant source of worry and anxiety. Now, think about what would happen to you if that fear came true—if your worries proved true. Does your blood pressure start to rise? If this happens, focus on remembering the truth that God is in control of everything. Even if our worst fears come true, it is because the God who loves you and is working in all things for your good has *allowed* them to come true. He's not surprised by the things you worry about; he's not shocked. He allowed these things to happen for a reason, and your response is to have faith in God in the midst of these circumstances. You can choose to love him and love others, secure in the fact that your reward is already secured for you by Jesus.

4. Working for Jesus gives you freedom to rest from your work. God rested after the sixth day of creation. God granted the Israelites rest from their enemies in the Promised Land. Jesus sat down at the right hand of the Father after his work on the cross. Our Creator is a gracious God who calls us, not to endless labor, but to a healthy rhythm of work and rest. Regular rest is a natural restraint that God has built into our lives. It's a gift that reminds us we are dependent on God and allows us to enjoy the fruit of our labors—even when our work on this earth feels endless!

Keeping rest in proper perspective is difficult, no matter

whether our tendency is to be idle in our work or to make work an idol. Idleness in work leads us to think that rest is the only thing that really matters. "I work so I can play," goes the slogan. This ignores God's purposes for our work. It's *not* just a means to the end of rest. God has purposes for us in our work itself. Rest is simply the reward that comes from a job well done.

When we idolize work, we resist rest. Rest becomes an irritant, a necessity that keeps us from achieving our goals, a reminder of our limitations. It's a speed bump on the road to success, a forced exile from what really matters. But here's the thing: God knows your limits. He designed them. You can trust him when he says you need to rest. Someone back in the early 1900s once remarked, "The graveyards are full of people the world could not do without." Do you think the world is going to collapse around you if you rest from your work? Is *your* life going to collapse? Are your dreams going to slip away? If you think so, even for a second, then you need to take that up with the God who created you and designed you with a need for rest. He designed you this way to teach you each night as you fall asleep that the things that matter most in life really don't depend on you and your work.

There are many ways to put into practice this truth about rest. First, set some natural boundaries. While you're at work, be focused, efficient, and intense. Once you leave, rest from your work. Don't check your work e-mail. Let your boss know how he or she can reach you in an emergency, but otherwise show restraint. You'll be back at work soon enough.

Second, bookend your days with prayers of dependence and thanks to God. In the morning, pray and ask him to give you wisdom to focus on the work he has for you. In the evening, thank God for the work he accomplished through you.

Third, set aside Sunday as a day of worship and rest—even if you fear that taking off an entire day will cost you profit or promotion. You may bear enormous responsibility in your work, but you need to recognize it is actually God who prospers your work—or declines to prosper it. God can grant success in surprising ways when we demonstrate our faith in him—even by *not* working!

5. Working for Jesus gives you freedom to do your work well. Studies show that the correlation between compensation and job performance is consistent—up to a point. Eventually, earning more money simply doesn't lead to better results. Once you have enough (whatever "enough" is for you), more money won't seem very enticing. The threat of getting fired won't hold much fear for you either. In other words, neither a carrot nor a stick will produce the best results. At some point, extrinsic motivation has to be replaced with intrinsic motivation. If you are doing your work for Jesus, you are free from the unsatisfying allure of the carrot and the painful whack of the stick. In doing your work for Jesus, you have the greatest intrinsic motivator you could ever have—the power of your desire to please him because of all he has done for you.

In the ancient Near East, working for the king was the highest calling one could have: "Do you see someone skilled in their work? They will serve before kings; they will not serve before officials of low rank" (Proverbs 22:29). Skilled work led to majestic service. Like Daniel, Nehemiah, Esther, and Mordecai, we also work for a king. In fact, we work for the King of kings. How much more, then, should our ethic, attitude, energy, effort, and excellence befit service to him! We should do good work simply because we work for the King.

6. Working for Jesus gives you freedom to have joy in your work. " 'Meaningless! Meaningless!' says the Teacher. 'Utterly meaningless! Everything is meaningless.' What do people gain from all their labors at which they toil under the sun?" (Ecclesiastes 1:2). Working for anyone other than Jesus is discouraging.

What's the point? We build something but leave it to someone else who might mess it up. We gain great fame but die, and no one remembers us. We save up for retirement but the market crashes, and we lose the promised rewards of hard work. We have a mundane, invisible job that seems pointless in the grand scheme of things. No wonder the teacher in Ecclesiastes threw up his hands in despair!

The answer to the fleetingness of life, though, is simple: Live your life with reference to the One who is not fleeting. The resurrection of Jesus clearly reveals why living your life for the Lord transforms everything. Your relationship with Jesus will last forever. Even if nobody notices you are working hard, *he notices*, and that means your work for him has eternal significance.

WHAT MAKES US DIFFERENT?

Ultimately, the evidence of the gospel in our lives at work is not so much in the things we do but in the freedom we enjoy in the midst of our work. To be sure, we should work ethically. We should honor our superiors. We should take satisfaction in a job well done. Those things are to be expected. But the truth is that they're not distinctively Christian. *Everyone* who works, not just Christians, should do these things.

As Christians, however, we have experienced something unique—something that those who don't know Jesus have not experienced. We know that no matter how hard we try, our attempts at pleasing God will always fall short. We know we are sinners undeserving of any blessing from God. Yet despite the hopelessness of our situation, we have heard and believe the good news that God has forgiven us! We don't fully know why, and we can barely even grasp how. But by God's grace and in his matchless love, we know we have been forgiven because of what Jesus the Messiah has done for us on the cross.

And that reality changes everything, including how we work.

You are now free. Free from the need to secure self-worth through performance. Free from the fear you will lose what is most precious to you if things don't go well. Free from a mad dash to work, work, work without any rest—as if the world depended on your effort. Free to work before the King with joy, even if it's not the work you would have chosen for yourself. Free to serve others as you worship the King.

It really is true. Working for Jesus changes ... *everything*.

1. Read and Reflect: Romans 6:18; Galatians 3:26–29; Matthew 22:34–40; Proverbs 22:29; Ecclesiastes 1:2–3

2. The most important thing about you as a worker is that you know Jesus. Why?

3. In what ways have you worshiped God through your work this past month? Think of two examples — one of how you learned to appreciate God more and one in which you grew in your obedience to God.

4. How does working for Jesus confront your idolatry of work? How does it confront your idleness at work?

5. Reread the Great Commandment in Matthew 22. How does this commandment from Jesus change the way you should think about and relate to your colleagues?

6. God created the Sabbath day as a day of rest. What does this say about how we should view our work?

7. Explain the basics of the gospel. How do these truths apply to your job?

CHAPTER 4

THE KING'S PURPOSES
IN OUR WORK

Work is not a source of ultimate satisfaction, nor is it a necessary evil. On the contrary, we should approach our jobs as if we are working for the King, and when we do, we experience a new freedom to work with joy and diligence, neither idolizing our jobs nor being idle in them.

Yet a question remains: Why does God want us to work in the first place? What are the King's purposes for us in our work? What does the Bible say should motivate us to get out of bed in the morning and do our jobs well?

Defining the purpose of work can be tricky. For example, is making money an acceptable reason to work, or is it wrong to do your work simply for a paycheck? Is sharing the gospel with our coworkers our primary reason for working, and if so, what do we do when company policy prohibits this? Different Christians will say different things when you ask them what motivates them to do their jobs. Some will say they go to work so they can give money to the church. Others will talk about their hope that the products of their work — whether physical, intellectual, or social—will have a lasting impact. Still others are motivated by the opportunity to interact with coworkers, build relationships with them, and share the gospel with them.

The Bible doesn't give us one single grand purpose to motivate us in our work. Instead, we are given multiple reasons, different motives, for working. Let's look at some of those purposes to see how they can motivate you to do your work with all your heart. Thinking through these points may help you answer the question we've all had at one time or another: "Why should I get up and go to work today?"

MOTIVATION #1: WORK TO LOVE GOD

Jesus said the greatest commandment is to "love the Lord your God with all your heart and with all your soul and with all your mind" (Matthew 22:37). Before anything else, we should love God in and through our jobs.

That's a revolutionary idea. It's hard to imagine a better motivator for working diligently and well, no matter where God has deployed us to work at this time. Think about Ephesians 6:5, 7 again: "Obey your earthly masters," Paul writes, "with respect and fear, and with sincerity of heart, just as you would obey Christ ... Serve wholeheartedly, as if you were serving the Lord, not people." Diligent, sincere, good work is to be motivated by our love for Jesus. Paul tells us that just as we would obey Christ "with respect and fear, and with sincerity of heart ... wholeheartedly," we should also serve those who employ us in a similar way—"with respect and fear, and with sincerity of heart ... wholeheartedly."

Your love for God should motivate you to work, no matter the particulars of what you do, "with your whole heart." If you are a mother, work at it with all your heart, as working for the Lord. If you are a student, work at it with all your heart, as working for the Lord. If you make cars, close sales, litigate, or medicate, do it as if you were working for the Lord himself—because you are! You love God; therefore work with all your heart!

MOTIVATION #2: WORK TO LOVE OTHERS

If loving God is the greatest commandment, Jesus tells us that right behind it is love for others: "Love your neighbor as yourself" (Matthew 22:39). Just as our love for God should motivate us to do our work well, so should our love for other people.

Why is that? It's simple, really. God has chosen to order the world in such a way that our food isn't just miraculously zapped into our refrigerators each day. Clothes do not grow on trees, nor do our houses assemble themselves. The trash we produce doesn't just magically disappear each evening. And human society doesn't naturally remain ordered. All of this happens through the process we call "work." And we love other people by helping make all of these things happen.

Consider the wisdom of Martin Luther on this subject: "When we pray the Lord's Prayer, we ask God to give us this day our daily bread. And he *does* give us our daily bread. He does it by means of the farmer who planted and harvested the grain, the baker who made the flour into bread, the person who prepared our meal."* Do you see what Luther is saying here? God provides for our needs through the work he calls us to do in and for the good of society.

Occasionally people will turn their noses up at the idea that there is purpose to be found in working to sustain society. After all, society is not eternal, right? We want our work to have *eternal* significance! However, we must remember that we human beings are created. We are creatures made by a Creator. And

---

*Cited in Gene Edward Veith Jr., *God at Work: Your Christian Vocation in All of Life* (Wheaton, Ill.: Crossway, 2002), 13.

since he is the Creator, God gets to decide what he wants us to do. God wants us as human beings to do things that are special and unique, so God has created some things for us to do that are unique to us. So, for example, God created angels, and he made them to stand in his presence, worship him, and be his messengers. They were designed for those specific purposes. Yet God (at least to our knowledge) *doesn't* want them to build a society on earth with things like angel grocery stores and angel real estate agencies. Evidently, that's not why he made angels. God *does* want human beings to do these things, however. He wants us to organize ourselves into societies in which order is maintained and systems are developed to sustain us. God takes pleasure in well-ordered societies, and he is glorified when we do our part to make this happen. When we give our time and ability to making and improving society, we are doing what God intended us as created human beings to do, even if the societies we create and sustain are not themselves eternal.

It's easy to talk in generalities—looking at all this from the macro level. But loving others typically happens not at this level but at the day-to-day micro level of relationships with individual people. We are called to love the particular people with whom we rub shoulders every day, and that ought to motivate us to do our work well. If you have a tendency to slack off at work, you may be saving yourself some stress and creating some ease in your life, but you're certainly not loving anybody else. In fact, you're probably creating more work for them because they'll have to pick up *your* slack!

When we realize we work in order to love others, it motivates us to work hard and work well, to encourage the people who work with us, and to strive not just for our own good but for the good of those around us. If you work only for yourself or only for your boss or only for your clients, then you are missing what is most important about your work. You are called to do what you do for *God's* purposes—so that you may love him and love others around you.

MOTIVATION #3: WORK TO REFLECT GOD'S CHARACTER

Believe it or not, part of the purpose and motivation for your work is to reflect God's own character to the world around us. When God created human beings, he created us "in [his] image, in [his] likeness" (Genesis 1:26). At the core, those phrases mean human beings had a God-given job to do in the world. They were to stand as God's representatives, ruling the world as his vice-regents and communicating to the universe, "It is God who rules!" As they did so, they would also reflect his character to the world.

In one way or another, your job somehow involves the work of bringing beauty out of ugliness, order out of chaos. Perhaps unassembled pieces are pulled together to make a widget used to create a product that people use. Or natural products are identified, isolated, and harvested to create something new. Sickness is treated; injustice is rectified; broken windows are repaired; cracked sidewalks are fixed. Even if your job is operating a wrecking ball, you probably aren't doing this just "to watch the world burn." You knock down old buildings for a purpose—to eventually make room for new ones!

All of this creative action in our work reflects the character and work of God. Think about it. Before God created the world, the universe was "formless and empty" (Genesis 1:2). There was nothing there! Everything was void and chaos. Over the next six days, God formed and filled the earth, purposefully bringing order and beauty out of the chaos of the void. Instead of darkness, God brought forth light. Instead of unformed waters, God created land and seas. Instead of nothingness or formlessness,

God made planets and stars and birds and trees and penguins and people. And at the end of it all, God looked at his work and saw that it was good—even *very* good! It's no accident, then, that when God finished his work and placed Adam in the garden of Eden, he called him also to work—to create order and beauty in the world. That is at least part of what God meant when he told Adam to subdue the earth and to work and take care of the garden (Genesis 1:28; 2:15). Yes, God had done the divine work of bringing beauty and order out of the void. Now he was calling Adam—his little image bearer—to carry the work even further by bringing about even more beauty and order. Like Father, like son!

Another way we reflect the character of God is in our exercise of authority. What does this look like? The Bible tells us that because God created everything, he is the ultimate authority over everything. When he created us, God decided to give us a measure of his authority as well—not unfettered autonomy, but a delegated authority, one that operates under his oversight and permission. When we use this authority wisely and respect the authority God has over us, we show the world around us that authority is designed to be a good thing. This is a truth that is generally not understood or respected in our contemporary culture. Most people think of authority as an evil thing, or at best as something we tolerate to maintain the social order.

Our jobs give us an opportunity to reject that lie. The Bible teaches us that even though authority can be corrupted, it is actually a good thing that operates under God's sovereign control. This is true whether we ourselves wield authority in our jobs or whether we must act under the authority of others. If you exercise authority over people in your job, do so in a godly, humble, loving, caring, and responsible way. The way you exercise authority will speak loudly to your employees, revealing not just *your* own authority but the way you submit to *God's* ultimate authority. In the same way, choose to live well under the authorities God has placed over you. If you are an employee, respect and honor those who are in authority over you. Don't communicate to people around you a spirit of rebellion, a sense that authority is somehow illegitimate or burdensome, a necessary evil to tolerate. Let them know by your actions that you consider good authority to be a blessing from God and that you understand all authority to be derived from him. In that way, you will reflect God's character, not only to your coworkers, but also to those who have authority over you.

MOTIVATION #4: WORK FOR MONEY

There is no reason to beat around the bush on this one. One of the main reasons we work is so we can provide for ourselves, our families, those we love, and others. We work so we can eat. Paul addresses this motivation in 2 Thessalonians 3:10: "The one who is unwilling to work shall not eat." Solomon writes in Proverbs 12:11, "Those who work their land will have abundant food, but those who chase fantasies have no sense." And Paul writes in Ephesians 4:28, "Anyone who has been stealing must steal no longer, but must work, doing something useful with their own hands, that they may have something to share with those in need."

It glorifies God when a Christian works hard to provide for his family and to be a blessing to others. It shows others that our contentment is grounded in God, not in the things of this world or in our own advancement. Therefore, you can take satisfaction and work with all your heart in a job that simply *provides*, even if it might not be the most personally fulfilling job you can imagine or the most financially lucrative job out there. Providing for your family, blessing others, supporting the work of the church—all of these are legitimate and good reasons to work.

This summarizes much of what Paul means when he states that Christians should "lead a quiet life" (1 Thessalonians 4:11). If God has called you to do your job simply to provide for your own needs and the needs of your family and to have opportunities to bless others and support the work of the church, then he has given you a valuable blessing and called you to do a very good thing.

This motivation — to work for money — is sometimes distasteful to people, especially to Christians. Some Christians grow discontented in their jobs because they think they're simply spinning their wheels if they're not passionate about what they are doing. They grumble and sigh deeply with every paycheck, because their work isn't "meaningful" enough for them. Yet this attitude expresses a discontent born of thinking that meaning and purpose in life should come primarily from our jobs. Because we have made our jobs into an idol, we pine for work that will give us the deeper meaning and purpose we long for. On the other hand, this discontent encourages us at the same time to grow idle in our work because we lose interest in doing what God has actually called us to do. We fail to see or grasp the purposes for which he has put us in our current situation. We struggle with *both* idolatry and idleness.

Our ultimate sense of meaning and purpose as Christians should come from knowing that everything we do is for Jesus' glory, which in turn should motivate us to work with all our heart wherever he has deployed us in this season of our lives. Aligning your job with your passions is great. And certainly, personal career growth is a good thing, and it is fine to pursue satisfaction in our jobs. However, none of those things should be the primary reason for our work. We work to glorify Jesus, no matter what we do. The Bible could not be clearer about this. And one of the ways we glorify Jesus is by our providing for our needs and then having enough left over to provide for the needs of others. The love of money may be "a root of all kinds of evil" (1 Timothy 6:10), but a godly use of money glorifies God.

MOTIVATION #5: WORK FOR ENJOYMENT

In his kindness, God even allows us to enjoy the fruits of our labors. Moses writes in Deuteronomy 8:18 that it is God "who gives you the ability to produce wealth." Paul writes in 1 Timothy 6:17 that God "richly provides us with everything for our enjoyment," and Ecclesiastes 5:18–19 even states, "It is appropriate for a person to eat, to drink, and to find satisfaction in their toilsome labor ... to accept their lot and be happy in their toil—this is a gift of God."

What a realistic and wonderful way of looking at our work! True, our work can be "toilsome," there is no doubt about that! Yet at the same time, God also graciously uses our work to bring us satisfaction and enjoyment. Keep in mind that this is really an astonishing and unexpected display of God's grace. Think about it. Our work is toilsome because God cursed it, and he did this because of our sin against him! This means the toil and sweat of work are part of his *curse* against us—it's his *punishment* for our rebellion against him. Yet in his love, God has decided we can have some measure of enjoyment even in what has been cursed! Yes, we will toil and sweat and grow frustrated in our work. But when we find a measure of satisfaction and enjoyment in what we do, we should be especially grateful!

Do you ever experience satisfaction or enjoyment in your work? If not, it might be worth thinking about why you don't. Do you lack enjoyment in your job because you idolize it, expecting it to do things for you that only Jesus can do? Or is it because you've lost sight of the purposes for which God has called you to work in the first place, and you've become idle in your work? You don't necessarily have to enjoy the *mechanics* of what you do in order to find a measure of enjoyment and satisfaction in your work. Maybe your job is cleaning out the grease pits in a hydraulics factory and you work in a non-air-conditioned metal warehouse in the brutal 110-degree heat of East Texas. Hardly anyone can be expected to enjoy the mechanics of that particular job. Yet if this describes your work, you can still find satisfaction and enjoyment in it by doing your job well and knowing you are doing it for the King's glory and as an expression of love for him.

Enjoying our work and finding satisfaction in it bring glory to God. Why? Doing so reveals that our hearts find their rest and joy and satisfaction ultimately in him, no matter what circumstances he has decided to deploy us in.

MOTIVATION #6: WORK TO ADORN THE GOSPEL OF JESUS CHRIST

Look at Titus 2:9 – 10:

> Teach slaves to be subject to their masters in everything, to try to please them, not to talk back to them, and not to steal from them, but to show that they can be fully trusted, so that in every way they will make the teaching about God our Savior attractive.

In this passage, Paul is instructing workers to work well and to do their work honestly. Why? "So that in every way they will make the teaching about God our Savior attractive." When we work in ways that reflect God's loving authority, creativity, excellence, and honor, our lives back up and support the gospel we confess with our lips.

The way we live will never fully communicate the good news of Jesus Christ to anyone; we must use words to share a verbal announcement of what God has done in history in the person of Jesus Christ. Yet the way we live *does* communicate something to people. It can either confirm or undermine what we say with our lips. People are pretty good at recognizing those who are more interested in themselves than in serving others, who care more about getting ahead than about loving and caring for the people they work with. If that's the aroma you are giving off at your job right now, then you are destroying your witness to Jesus long before the gospel message ever crosses your lips. Be the aroma of Christ in your workplace. Adorn the gospel; don't sabotage it!

WORK IN FAITH

No matter what you do or how much you like your job (or don't like it), the most important thing is to do your work in faith—faith in God and in his plan for you and for this world.

If your tendency is to idolize your job, then consider if your faith in God is lacking. Is it possible that you are trusting more in yourself and your own abilities than in God and his promises to you? Could it be that, deep down, you really do believe that your success, your satisfaction, your future—they all depend on you? If so, we want to offer a little encouragement.

I (Seb) have struggled with this for most of my adult life. Through hard experience, I've settled on a work motto, a saying I repeat to myself to help me in my fight against making my work an idol.

Work hard, work smart, and trust God.

The last two words of this motto remind me how I can fight idolatry of my work. When I say this, I remember that no matter how hard and how smart I work, all of my accomplishments have the unmistakable finger of God on them. I may work harder and smarter than ever before, and my plans may still fail. At the same time, even though everything may look like it's headed for disaster, God can still surprise me and bring it all to success! Proverbs 19:21 confirms this: "Many are the plans in a person's heart, but it is the LORD's purpose that prevails." This means I should work with all my heart and at the same time keep my heart's trust firmly rooted in God. So work hard, work smart, and, above all, trust God!

This is also true if your tendency is to be idle in your work. One of our touchstone Bible verses addresses this: "Whatever you do, work at it with all your heart, as working for the Lord, not for human masters, since you know that you will receive an inheritance from the Lord as a reward. It is the Lord Christ you are serving" (Colossians 3:23 – 24). How do you encourage yourself to work with all your heart? By *knowing* that you work for the Lord, not for people. By *knowing* that Jesus has set apart an inheritance for you as a reward. That's an act of faith! It requires you to exercise a deep trust in Jesus, believing he knows what he is doing when he deploys you to work in a certain place. Rarely do we see the big picture of our life. Who *knows* why God wants you to be here doing this for this season of your life? And yet we can trust that he does, that he has deployed you here, as your King, and now it's your job to serve him faithfully where he has placed you for as long as he decides to keep you there.

In some ways, it can be helpful to have the mind-set of a soldier in an army. A soldier does what his general commands, even if he doesn't fully understand why he is deployed to a certain location or how his particular task fits in with the overall battle plan. Christians, in their work, need to learn to be content to serve as a private — an ordinary soldier — among God's people. We all want to be generals and tank commanders. We feel miffed when the King doesn't explain everything to us and simply decides to deploy us to the trenches. But isn't that his right? Isn't it a gift of incredible grace that we're on his side at all? Who are we, then, to accept grace from his hand, join his army, and then walk away sulking and kicking at the dirt when our King says, "And now, dear child, I want you to work over there in the trenches. I have a brilliant strategy that's unfolding, and I want you to work there for a while." People whose hearts are full of faith and love toward the King won't reject the King's commands. They'll jump toward their assignment with shouts of joy, knowing they are on a personal assignment for the King of kings!

So remember that no matter what you do, whether you're a private, a cook, a lieutenant, a latrine cleaner, a trench digger, or a tank commander, it is the King himself who has deployed you to that job. It's his call. You don't deserve to be in his army in the first place. You deserve to be crushed by it. Wherever he's decided to deploy you, trust him and serve him well. It isn't *what* you're doing that really matters...

It's *who* you're doing it for.

1. Read and Reflect: Ephesians 6:5 – 7; Genesis 1:26; 2 Thessalonians 3:10; Proverbs 12:11; 1 Timothy 6:17 – 19; Ecclesiastes 5:18 – 20; Titus 2:9 – 10; Proverbs 19:21

2. Christians have many good, biblical motives for work. Which motive in this chapter do you currently reflect on the least often? Why is it hard for you? Pray that God will help grow that motive in your heart this month.

3. Authority in the workplace — whether you exercise it or live under it — is often misunderstood or mishandled. How does working under God's authority reshape your attitude, whether you are a boss or report to a boss?

4. How does your specific work accomplish God's purposes for others? Give examples for your family, your church, your company, your coworkers, your customers, and society at large.

5. Reflect on each motive listed in this chapter and reread what the Bible says about each motive. Does reflecting on these motives help your heart be more content? How can knowing and believing each of these help your heart be more content?

CHAPTER 5

HOW SHOULD I CHOOSE A JOB?

Let's turn now to some specific thorny problems that can arise as we do our work. How, practically, does this biblical perspective on work apply to our day-to-day jobs? How do we find the right balance between our work, our family, and our involvement in the church? How do we deal with difficult bosses and competitive coworkers? What does it mean to be "successful"?

Before we jump into answering any of these questions, we want to start with an even more basic question: How do I choose a job? What does the Bible have to say about the process of choosing a career path or deciding to pursue a particular calling in my work?

First of all, we should acknowledge that the entire idea of "choosing" a job is largely a modern Western concept. For most of human history, work was something you did to survive, and often there were no options to consider. Most of the time, you did what your father or mother did, and that was the end of the story.

That's not to say we are the only people in history to face

this question; it's just that the options available to us today are greater than they were in the past. Specialization, mobility, and education have opened up the world to us in a way that most people in history have never experienced. The breakneck pace of technological advancement and the resulting disruption of industries mean that "choosing a job" is likely something most of us will do multiple times in our lives.

Choosing a job is rarely easy. It's difficult to find a good match for our skills, desires, and needs, and it is complicated by the fact that more people than ever are competing for the same jobs. We may find that technology has outstripped our skills and we will need to start over or learn something new to remain competitive. As Christians, we also have to wrestle with our hearts and our motives.

IDOLATRY AND IDLENESS IN CHOOSING A JOB

It is frighteningly easy to fall into idolatry in the process of choosing a job. We make an idol of choosing a job when we base our criterion for "the right job" on bringing glory and honor to ourselves rather than on bringing honor and glory to God. When we focus on the salary or status a job might bring us, we are in danger of falling into idolatry in our job search.

It's also possible to fall into the trap of idleness in seeking a job. We fall into idleness when we fail to see God's good purposes for work. Practically, this means we fail to exercise discernment; we fail to pray and seek God's counsel in our job search; we decide that any job will do. We may even resent the fact we have to search for a job, and so we put in little effort toward the search.

Both of those mind-sets are obviously wrong. So how do we avoid these ways of thinking? How can we cultivate a mind-set that resists the world's patterns and adheres to a biblical, gospel-shaped perspective? The answer is that we need to begin with God. As trite as this may sound at first, the fact is that most Christians *don't* begin their job searches with God and God's priorities; they begin with themselves.

Here's what we mean. Think of your decision-making process as a pyramid, wide and strong at the bottom, pointy and fairly crumbly at the top. A pyramid is amazingly stable as long as the strong part remains on the bottom and the weak part remains on the top—that is, when we base our lives and decisions on our highest, strongest priorities. Turn it over and try to rest the pyramid on the pointy part, though, and you have an immediate disaster on your hands! If that's true, then it's really important we keep our priorities properly ordered.

And what's the right order? Well, it goes like this: Obeying and Loving God on the bottom, Serving Others in the middle, and Pleasing Ourselves on the top.

A mind-set built on a biblical worldview is the only one that is stable enough and strong enough to hold up the weight of our lives. This reflects the way Jesus taught us to think as well. The greatest commandment (the base of the pyramid of our lives) is to "love the Lord your God." After that? To "love your neighbor as yourself." This means that "self" comes last. Self sits at the top of the pyramid—not because of its importance but because of its weakness. It simply can't bear the weight of a life created to honor God.

So what does it mean, practically, to keep God's priorities as the base of our decision making when searching for a job? We've developed six key questions you should ask yourself as you consider potential job opportunities. And we've ordered these questions in a very specific way.

The first three questions are what we call "must-haves." They're the questions to which, as Christians, we really must be able to answer yes for a job opportunity to be a real option for us. They're the questions that rest at the base of the pyramid. The last three questions are what we call "nice-to-haves." They're the questions that belong higher up on the pyramid — the things that are great if you can get them but aren't necessary in a job.

The Must-Haves

1. Does this job glorify God? Is what I would be doing in this job honoring to the Lord, or does it dishonor and disobey him? Here we have to exclude lines of work that would be inherently sinful. Working as a hit man, a drug runner, or a staff member at an abortion clinic dishonors God and is forbidden for a Christian. Of course, things aren't always quite that clear! Lines can be blurry, and people's consciences will feel differently about different lines of work. In general, though, it's important to start here. We want to do work that glorifies and honors God.

2. Does this job permit me to live a godly life? In other words, will this job allow me to obey God in every area of my life, or will it mean I have to sacrifice obedience in other areas? Will this job allow me to love my spouse well and parent my children well? Will this job force me to default on another biblical obligation? Will it allow me to obey God by having a rich, textured relationship with a church? If a job necessarily means we'll have to disobey God in other areas of our lives, then in all likelihood it's a job we should remove from consideration.

3. Does this job provide for my needs and allow me to be a blessing to others? Scripture commands us to be hard at work in order to provide for ourselves and our families and be generous toward those in need. We place this in the must-haves because it really is not an optional characteristic. Paul wrote in 1 Timothy 5:8, "Anyone who does not provide for their relatives, and especially for their own household, has denied the faith and is worse than an unbeliever." Wow! That's pretty clarifying, isn't it? If you choose a job that uses your gifts but doesn't pay enough to provide the basics for yourself and your family, the Bible says you're living in sin. Believe it or not, money is a must-have.

The Nice-to-Haves

4. Does this job benefit society in some way? Almost certainly, if you answered yes to the first three questions, you're going to answer yes to this one as well. The challenge is that it can be incredibly hard to quantify what qualifies as a benefit to society. We need to be very careful when trying to decide which of two jobs benefits society the most. For example, it can be easy to assume that nonprofit jobs benefit society more than sales jobs. But is that necessarily true? Think about it this way. Who provided the greater benefit to society through their life's work—Bill Gates or Mother Teresa? It's almost impossible to give a clear answer to that question. The world is too complex and there are too many variables for us to say, "This job is more beneficial than that one."

Still, we should at least consider the question. Is this job good? Does it seem beneficial to others, to the people around you? It may be challenging to compare the social benefits of various jobs, but it is still worth considering.

5. *Does this job take advantage of my gifts and talents?* Is this something that lines up with the gifts and abilities God has given me? The fact is, not everyone has the freedom to choose the kind of work they're going to do. Many people simply do what is available to them. If you have the luxury to consider this, though, it is preferable to work in a job you know you will be good at doing. The Bible is full of stories about God equipping people to do specific work. Bezalel was specially gifted to build the tabernacle, Joseph to administrate Pharaoh's kingdom, Daniel to govern, and David to be a warrior-poet. Sometimes God intends for our jobs to line up perfectly with the gifts and talents he's given us.

Sometimes.

Of course, there are other examples in the Bible where there doesn't seem to be any particular correspondence at all between a person's greatest gifts and his daily job. The Bible never tells us that Paul was an especially gifted maker of tents. He may have simply done this work to support himself. Was Peter a world-renowned talent at fishing? Apparently, he had plenty of days when the nets were empty. Was Moses just *made* to stand in front of a king and speak boldly to him? No way! Yet God called him to do it anyway. Here's the point. It's great to have a job that lines up with what you perceive to be your gifts and talents. By all means, *do it* if the opportunity arises! God may give you a job that aligns with your gifts, but he certainly hasn't promised to do so. Practically, then, you shouldn't make this a must-have in your decision making.

6. *Is this job something I* want *to do?* You should have realistic, biblical expectations about the level of satisfaction and fulfillment a job will bring. The world often tells us that finding a job you enjoy is *the* key aim in life. But the Bible says nothing of the sort; it simply states, "*Whatever you do*, work at it with all your heart, as working for the Lord, not for human masters" (Colossians 3:23, emphasis added). It's nice to have a job you really enjoy, and that should be a consideration in choosing a job. At the same time, be careful that "enjoyment" doesn't become your all-consuming priority. Thinking this way is really just another way of making ourselves the highest priority.

Take another look at the pyramid of priorities. As you work through these six questions, you're making your way *up* the pyramid. These questions should lead you to start with God, then consider others, and finally think about yourself. That's the kind of mind-set that will lead to a stable, godly decision-making process.

Most people—even Christians—don't think like this at all. In fact, they completely invert the pyramid.

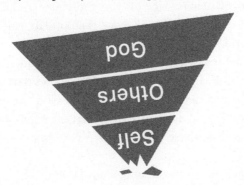

They start their job search by asking the question, "What do *I* want to do?" Only then do they ask whether a job will benefit others, and finally they do a quick check to make sure they're not about to sin when they sign on the dotted line.

Inverted thinking leads to all kinds of problems. It amplifies our tendency to think first of ourselves, which distorts the way we think about what kind of job might be best for us. If we start with selfish considerations, we may find ourselves wrongly ruling out jobs that would honor God perfectly well; allow us to live quiet, godly lives; provide for our needs; and allow us to benefit others. In the same way, inverted thinking can lead us to jump at a job that might be fulfilling to us in its own way but doesn't pay enough to support us. It can lead to employment that makes demands on us that force us to shirk other responsibilities or to a job that doesn't really benefit anyone but ourselves. When we invert the pyramid and expect concerns of self to bear the weight of our decision making, the whole process becomes hopelessly unstable.

So how do you make a decision about which job to choose? Very simply, you start at the bottom of the pyramid and work your way up. Which jobs available to you will glorify God? Which of those will best allow you to live a godly life? Which ones will adequately provide for you and your family? Which will benefit others? Which of those that are left will best fit your gifts and fulfill your desires? Which one will you enjoy most? Sometimes by the time you get through question 4 or 5, there's just one option left. That's OK. Don't pass up a job that *isn't* personally fulfilling yet glorifies God and provides for your family. And don't pick a job that *is* personally fulfilling if it doesn't do those basic things. Keep the pyramid right side up!

Of course, there's one other obvious point to keep in mind. If God doesn't give you an opportunity to do a certain thing, then he's not calling you to do that thing, at least not now. God directs our steps through *present* opportunities. There is nothing wrong with thinking about options and considering "What ifs." Yet we still have to do what God puts in front of us *today*. Solomon wrote two nearly identical proverbs about this truth. Proverbs 12:11 reads, "Those who work their land will have abundant food, but those who chase fantasies have no sense." Proverbs 28:19 reads, "Those who work their land will have abundant food, but those who chase fantasies will have their fill of poverty." This is such a practical and important point that Solomon says it twice! Don't chase fantasies. Take advantage of the opportunities you have right now instead of dreaming fancifully about opportunities you may never have.

CONCLUSION

There is no simple equation that will always lead you to find the best job. These questions are simply meant to help you develop a framework for thinking about what is most important, which opportunities should be ruled out, and which ones you should be pursuing. The principles laid out in this chapter are not determinative, but we hope they are helpful.

Choosing a job is a pretty important life decision, and it's one that should be made with earnest prayer, biblical study, and wise counsel from other Christians. Finally, it's a decision for which you should set aside ample — *but not endless* — time. In his book *The 4-Hour Workweek*, Tim Ferriss advocates quick decision making if the decisions are nonfatal and reversible. Though the decision to pursue a certain career path or accept a particular job offer can feel at the time like the most important decision we'll ever make, the truth is that they are subject to change as well. This means we should exercise wisdom, pray, seek counsel, plan, and strategize, and then we should make a decision quickly and move on. Why? Because in the final analysis God is in control. He is sovereign over everything — and that certainly extends to our jobs! We can place our lives and our careers in his hands, knowing he is a good and kind King who works all things for his glory and our good. He will not waste our deployment.

So above all else, trust in God as you choose a job. Jobs are temporary; God is eternal. If it looks like you may have to choose a job that isn't perfect for you, praise God and do it with all your heart. One day that job will end. And if it looks like you've landed the job of your dreams, work at it with all your heart. Remember, one day it, too, will end! Either way, you work for Jesus. You can trust he has good reasons for the work he is giving you to do.

1. Read and Reflect: 1 Timothy 5:8; Proverbs 12:11; Proverbs 28:19

2. Think about your last job change. What must-haves did you have as you evaluated that job? How do those align with Scripture?

3. How does the list of considerations in this chapter influence your thinking about your next job? Your career track? How does this list compare with what your colleagues think would be the next "smart move" for your career?

4. Which nice-to-have consideration are you tempted to sinfully elevate to must-have status? Why?

5. When we consider changing jobs, our culture often encourages us to talk with a career coach, a mentor, or a professional recruiter. Those are all good things to do. What other things might a Christian do to seek counsel in this decision?

6. "Work hard, work smart, and trust God." In what ways have you seen God's fingerprints on your life and career?

CHAPTER 6

HOW DO I BALANCE WORK, CHURCH, AND FAMILY?

It was 3:00 a.m., and I (Seb) was curled up on a hospital room couch. It was just a few hours after I welcomed my first child into the world, and I could not sleep. My inability to sleep wasn't due to the overwhelming joy and excitement of having a child. In fact, it was the opposite problem—I was terrified! How was I going to be able to do it all? I was barely keeping my head above water with all the work that comes from being a husband, church member, and businessman. Now I just added a new, über-important "to do" to my crowded list of responsibilities: I was a father with a child to care for in our home for at least the next eighteen years. How on earth was I going to do it all?

I came to a solution. I decided I could fail at my job. It was the only responsibility in my life that seemed flexible. I knew I couldn't fail as a disciple of Jesus. I couldn't fail as a husband or as a father. That left one option. I would do the best I could at work, but if something had to give, it would have to be my work.

Still, it wasn't a perfect solution. After all, I now had a family to support. So I had to "succeed" at my job, at least well enough to put food on the table, or I'd end up failing my family. Yet I still decided that if I had to fail somewhere, I'd fail at my job.

Is this really the answer to balancing our responsibilities? Does God really give us multiple assignments and expect us to pick the one he wants us to fail at? If not, how do you balance it all without failing? How do you remain fruitful and faithful at work when you also need to be fruitful and faithful as a spouse, parent, neighbor, and church member? How do you do it all in the mere 168 hours that comprise a week?

The area of balancing responsibilities is tightly related to the issues we've been discussing in this book. On the one hand, we don't want to be idle at work. We can't throw up our hands and decide work doesn't matter. After all, God intends us to work, and he intends us to work *for him*. Whatever we do, we should do it with all our heart. Failing at our jobs isn't the solution. On the other hand, we can't declare that our jobs are of the utmost importance and be content to fail in our other responsibilities. We can't sacrifice God-given responsibilities on the altar of work.

How do you do it all? That's the question, isn't it? Failing anywhere in the assignments God has given is not really an option. So is it possible to keep all the balls juggling in the air? As in most of life, there's no equation that magically solves this problem. There's no way to make it easy. But remembering that we are disciples of Jesus above all and that we work for him in everything we do helps us to be faithful and fruitful in *all* of the responsibilities he has given us, not just *some* of them.

OUR ONE AND ONLY FIRST RESPONSIBILITY — DISCIPLESHIP TO JESUS

We tend to think of our various responsibilities as somewhat unrelated to each other, like a set of balls we're trying to juggle. Sure, we may see some relationship between them. For example, our jobs provide money for support of our families and our church, and we take our families to church with us. But we also tend to see our responsibilities as being in competition with one another, especially for the limited amount of time and energy we have in a given week. And so we will often set our various responsibilities against each other, which leads to a feeling of constant tension between them instead of viewing them as working together in harmony.

The Bible doesn't depict the responsibilities of life as a juggling act. In fact, Scripture is clear that we have one primary assignment and that everything else is subordinate to it. What is that primary assignment? It is our calling to follow Jesus. The Bible makes this point in a number of different ways.

Jesus states in Matthew 6:33, "Seek first his kingdom and his righteousness, and all these things will be given to you as well." There is a clear logic in this statement. Jesus tells us we have one primary responsibility, and when we do that well, everything else we need will be provided. In other words, everything else fits under and is organized by the one overarching responsibility we have, namely, to follow Jesus.

In his book *The Call*, Os Guinness gives a great explanation of why following Jesus must be our primary responsibility. He says it is necessarily first because as believers our lives are *by* him, *to* him, and *for* him. Consider what Paul writes in 2 Thessalonians 2:14: "He called you to this [salvation] through our gospel." Who called you? Jesus did. So you have been called to salvation *by* Jesus.

Now look at John 17:6 to see how Jesus prays for those who believe in him: "I have revealed you to those whom you gave me out of the world. They were yours; you gave them to me." To whom do you belong? To Jesus. God gave you *to* him. If you're a Christian, you might as well have a sticker on your forehead that reads, "To Jesus, from your Father!"

Finally, read what Paul writes in Ephesians 2:10: "We are God's handiwork, created in Christ Jesus to do good works, which God prepared in advance for us to do." What are we to do now that we've been saved? Good works that will redound to the glory of Jesus. We are to live *for* him.

Do you see how comprehensive this calling to follow Jesus really is? We have been saved *by* Jesus; we are given *to* Jesus; and now we are called to live *for* Jesus. Discipleship to him must be our primary, overarching, undergirding assignment. It happened before every other assignment, supersedes every other assignment, and will last long after every other assignment is complete.

Your discipleship to Jesus is not just one more ball flying around in your life. It is not in competition with other responsibilities. It is your first responsibility, and all others are defined by it. Think back again to Colossians 3:23. (You probably have it memorized by now!) Why are we to work with all our heart at whatever we do? Because we do whatever we do "for the Lord"! Our first and greatest responsibility organizes and defines all the secondary "whatever you do" responsibilities. Church life, family life, and work life fall under the "whatever you dos" — those secondary responsibilities we have as humans and Christians. They are the arenas in which we live out our primary calling to follow Jesus and bring him honor and glory. Are you in school? God has given you the assignment right now of being a student who is striving to follow Jesus and bring him glory. Are you a husband? God has assigned you the work of being a husband who is striving to follow Jesus and bring him glory. Are you a retiree? God has called you to be a retiree who is striving to follow Jesus and bring him glory. Are you unemployed right now? Even then, you need to understand your assignment from God, right now, is to be unemployed. And he intends for you to use that season to follow Jesus and bring him glory.

FAITHFULNESS AND FRUITFULNESS IN FAMILY, CHURCH, AND WORK

The chaos of balancing our lives begins to clear up when we understand we have one primary responsibility. Our various callings and duties in life are no longer in direct competition with one another because they are all subsumed under that overriding responsibility of following Christ. But this doesn't mean the pressure is gone. We will often feel the pressure of our secondary responsibilities bumping into one another, even when we understand they are subservient to this primary goal.

So, for example, how should we spend an unexpected free afternoon? Should we finish a work project early, spend time with the kids, or do some kind of ministry at church? There are no pat, simple answers to these questions. In fact, the answers will be different for different situations and different individuals. Instead of answering this question definitively, we want to suggest some principles that can help you manage the jostling demands of family, church, and work.

For every assignment in your life, you will find in the Bible both a minimum standard for *faithfulness* and principles for pursuing further *fruitfulness*. By a minimum standard for faithfulness, we mean the basic requirements Scripture gives in an area of our calling. If you are failing to live up to these basic standards in one of your assignments, then you are not being faithful in that area. Most of the time, this means you need to double-down on your attention there before looking anywhere else.

By principles for pursuing further fruitfulness, we mean those ways in which we can grow beyond this minimum expectation of faithfulness. Once you think you're meeting the Bible's standard of faithfulness in all your assignments, you are free to dream and consider how you can best invest your extra time and energy.

On either side of faithfulness and fruitfulness we will find the two pitfalls that tend to define the sinful patterns associated with our work—idolatry and idleness. Fail to meet the minimum requirement of faithfulness, and you fall into idleness. Push beyond fruitfulness, and you fall into idolatry.

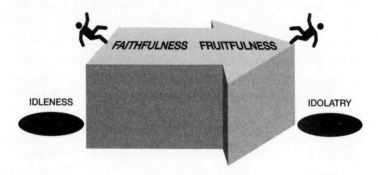

So here's the guiding principle: pursue faithfulness, then fruitfulness, but *not* idolatry. You might want to memorize that! It's a simple way to think about how to best manage the complex assignments God has given you.

1. Determine if you're being faithful in your assignments.
2. Consider where you might be able to invest for greater fruitfulness.
3. Avoid the trap of idolatry, where you are mastered by your work instead of serving the Lord.

Faithfulness. Then fruitfulness. But not idolatry.

Let's consider how this guiding principle impacts our secondary assignments of family, church, and work.

Family

What is the minimum standard of faithfulness when it comes to your family? In all honesty, it's probably higher than you think! According to Ephesians 5:22, 25, faithfulness in your family is a pretty high bar: "Wives, submit yourselves to your own husbands, as you do to the Lord ... Husbands, love your wives, just as Christ loved the church and gave himself up for her." Entire books have been written about how this works out in real life. The standard of faithfulness is self-sacrifice in the forms of loving, godly submission for wives and of self-denying love for husbands.

If you have children, the standard of faithfulness is also quite high: "Fathers,... bring [your children] up in the nurture and admonition of the Lord" (Ephesians 6:4 KJV). When it comes to your family, the minimum standard of faithfulness isn't all that minimum, is it? Wives are to submit to their husbands as the church submits to Christ. Husbands are to love their wives as Christ loved the church. And both are to raise their children to fear the Lord and obey his commandments.

Husbands and wives can also invest in each other and their children in order to maximize fruitfulness. Some husbands and wives invest time in retreats with each other or getaways with the kids. Some spend extra money on family experiences; others spend it on other equally valuable things. The fact is that nothing in Scripture commands us to take family vacations or schedule regular "family days." As long as we're being faithful to Scripture's already-high standard of faithfulness, those kinds of things are not strictly necessary. They're investments of extra resources into our families with the intention of maximizing fruitfulness in that arena of our lives.

Of course, it's also worth realizing that faithfulness and fruitfulness in family life isn't going to work itself out in exactly the same way for every person. Different people will have to be wise about determining the level of emotional, spiritual, and physical support your spouse and children require. Don't try to define what *faithful* or *fruitful* means for you by comparing your family life to others'. Determine it rather by considering how the Bible's commands and principles intersect with the real, specific, and providential circumstances of your life.

Is it possible for a person to wrongly idolize his wife or his children? Sure! There are two ways this can happen. First, if your investment of time and attention into your family causes you to fall below the Bible's standard of faithfulness in other areas of your life, you've wrongly elevated the importance of your family. If you simply declare you're not going to work at all because you want to spend every waking hour of your life with your kids, you're not being faithful in the arena of work. Similarly, if you decide to take two Sundays a month to skip the gathering of your church and play soccer with your kids, you're not being faithful in your responsibility to be committed to a church. Even more fundamentally, however, Jesus himself set the threshold of idolatry when it comes to family. He said, "Anyone who loves their father or mother more than me is not worthy of me; anyone who loves their son or daughter more than me is not worthy of me" (Matthew 10:37). If you love your family more than you love Jesus, then you've crossed the threshold of idolizing your family.

Church

What about your involvement in the church and your relationships with others in the body of Christ? According to the Bible, the minimum standard of faithfulness when it comes to church seems to be that every Christian should be meaningfully committed to the life of a local church community. Over and over, the New Testament seems to assume every believer will be meaningfully connected to and committed to a church. Paul writes to the believers in the local church at Corinth, "Now you are the body of Christ, and each one of you is a part of it" (1 Corinthians 12:27). A local church is a body, and each person is a member of that body and contributes to its well-being. Hebrews 10:24–25 makes it clear that it's not enough just to be *theoretically* committed to a church. We should "spur one another on toward love and good deeds" — "not giving up meeting together," the author of Hebrews states, and "encouraging one another." The minimum standard of faithfulness here is a meaningful commitment to a local church — a commitment that leads us to meet together regularly with that church and be actively involved in encouraging, loving, and urging on the other members of that church.

Depending on your life's circumstances at the moment, you may find that God is calling you to invest more time, energy, and attention into maximizing your service and even your leadership within the church. Not everyone is called to be an elder in the church. Yet some people will be called to this, and Paul implies that having a desire to be an elder is a good desire (see 1 Timothy 3:1). You don't have to give up an extra night each week to lead a ministry in order to be a faithful member of your church, but it could be a very good thing for you to do in order to maximize your fruitfulness in the life of the church. Every Christian needs to be a member of the church, but we aren't all the same member with the same level of commitment. Each of us plays the role God has given us — whether as an eye, an ear, or a fingernail.

And yes, it is possible to turn your service and leadership in the church into an idol. If your investment of time and energy in your church causes you to default on being faithful in your other God-given obligations, then you've idolized the church, and you need to reassess things. In fact, Paul seems to be addressing this idolizing of the ministry in 1 Corinthians 3:5–9:

> What, after all, is Apollos? And what is Paul? Only servants, through whom you came to believe — as the Lord has assigned to each his task. I planted the seed, Apollos watered it, but God has been making it grow. So neither the one who plants nor the one who waters is anything, but only God, who makes things grow. The one who plants and the one who waters have

one purpose, and they will each be rewarded according to their own labor. For we are co-workers in God's service; you are God's field, God's building.

We must guard against thinking that our ministry in the church is somehow indispensable. No matter what you do in the body of Christ, you are still only watering and planting. Only God makes things grow. Forget that, and you've wandered across the threshold of idolatry.

Work

The Bible also gives us parameters of faithfulness, fruitfulness, and idolatry for our work life. The minimum standard of faithfulness for our work is really pretty simple. First Thessalonians 4:10–12 reads, "We urge you, brothers and sisters, . . . to make it your ambition to lead a quiet life. You should mind your own business and work with your hands, just as we told you, so that your daily life may win the respect of outsiders and so that you will not be dependent on anybody." Ephesians 4:28 puts it like this: "Anyone who has been stealing must steal no longer, but must work, doing something useful with their own hands, that they may have something to share with those in need." The minimum threshold in the arena of work is to be able to provide for ourselves, take care of our families, and have something left over to share with others. That's it!

You can always invest more time, energy, and attention into a job in order to maximize your talents and abilities for the glory of God and the good of others. You can give a few more hours or spend a little more brain space strategizing and planning. You can offer to travel for your employer or take a promotion that utilizes your gifts better but also requires a little more time. None of that is strictly necessary to be faithful in your job, no matter what the world may tell you. But those things may be a great way to invest some of the extra resources of your life.

Work becomes an idol when our investment of resources runs out of "extra" and starts encroaching on our other areas of responsibility. The threshold of idolatry when it comes to work is well-defined by Solomon when he states, "Do not wear yourself out to get rich; have the wisdom to show restraint" (Proverbs 23:4 NIV, 1984 ed.). Solomon talks about getting rich, but we can easily substitute other ideas there as well. Don't wear yourself out to get satisfaction. Don't wear yourself out to get influence. Don't wear yourself out to get power. Don't wear yourself out to get respect. Don't wear yourself out to get stuff. If you fail to restrain yourself, you've crossed the threshold into idolatry of work.

PULLING IT ALL TOGETHER

God has given us a number of assignments in our lives. He expects us to be neither idle nor idolatrous in any of them, but to begin by pursuing faithfulness and adding fruitfulness when we can in each of these callings.

It's a little too easy to talk about our responsibilities clinically and neatly, as if each one fits tightly into its own custom-made carrying case. In the real world, things are never that neat. We live in a world where things come up and life happens—whether we want it to or not. We're trying to be faithful at work, and a child gets sick. We're trying to be faithful at home, and a church member calls with a crisis. The goalposts move; the target jumps around. And before we know it, we can find ourselves discouraged, distracted, and overwhelmed.

That was the way I (Seb) thought about my life after my son was born! Instinctively, I was trying to relieve the pressure I was feeling by running from one of my God-given assignments. "I'll just default on my work." I convinced myself that failing would be necessary to be faithful to God in other areas of my life. But I was wrong. All of these assignments are given to us by God.

Therefore, we can be sure he wants us to be faithful in them and, in increasing measure, to be fruitful as well.

We shouldn't fool ourselves into thinking there's a one-size-fits-all solution to all this. If we just had a divine checklist, we could do that pretty easily. But we don't. Instead, God has simply given us broad parameters of what too much looks like (idolatry) and what too little looks like (idleness). And he calls us to exercise godly wisdom to figure out when and where more investment will yield greater fruitfulness.

With this in mind, here is some practical advice to guide your thinking:

1. Determine what it means to be faithful in each of your assignments. Write out a job description for each of the assignments the Lord has given you in your life. What does it mean to be faithful in your family life, your church life, and your job life? The world has its own ideas of what a "minimum standard" would look like for each. As Christians we should define these things from the Bible as it intersects with our particular circumstances.

2. Evaluate yourself with regard to each of those assignments and what it means to be faithful in them. Ask yourself hard questions. If you have a lot of free time on your hands, why is that? Are you being unfaithful in one of your assignments? Are you failing to invest in one of them where you could maximize your fruitfulness? On the other hand, if you're struggling to keep your head above water, why is that? Is your job too difficult for you? Are you trying to climb the ladder too quickly? Are you saying yes to too many service opportunities at church? Are you being faithful to rest, as God has commanded you to do? Has one of your assignments become an idol to you? Self-evaluation of this sort doesn't have to be lonely. If you're married, ask your spouse to help you think through it. If not, ask a close friend who knows you well. Don't let yourself be fooled into thinking this is merely a matter of hours spent. It's not. You can spend fewer hours at work and still be completely emotionally disconnected from your family because you've made an idol of your job and let it dominate your mind.

3. Repent of any sin you discover. If you've discovered you're being idle in one or more of your assignments, repent. Look back at what you wrote down about what Scripture says is the standard of faithfulness and determine to meet it, starting immediately! At the same time, if you discover that one of your assignments has become an idol, repent of that too. Remember, these things tend to come in pairs. Idleness in one area will often point to idolatry in another, and vice versa. Whatever you discover, though, here's the point: identify how you've overemphasized or underemphasized one or more of your responsibilities. Make adjustments quickly to bring them all back into line with your first responsibility of following and honoring Jesus.

4. Consider where you might press forward in fruitfulness in one or all of your assignments. Is there anywhere you can invest a little more time and energy to increase your fruitfulness in a particular area? For example, maybe it's time to consider leading a ministry in your church or becoming a Bible study leader. Maybe you've built up some flexibility in your job that you could use to spend extra time with your spouse. Maybe the moment has come when you can finally consider applying for that promotion. Maybe there's no margin at all. As long as you're being faithful in all your assignments, there's no need to feel guilty. If life is full, then life is full. Live faithfully every day, and trust God to open up space in your life when he is ready!

CONCLUSION

Different circumstances will require different strategies and different decisions. For that reason, evaluating your life and assignments ought to be more than just a once-a-decade thing. You should do it regularly so you can make sure you don't lose sight of what it means to be faithful in all your areas of responsibility. Avoid the mistake of looking at someone else's life and judging yourself by that standard. The standard of faithfulness defined by Scripture may be similar for different people, but you can't just look at your friend's decision to invest extra time as an elder in the church and conclude that faithfulness requires you to do the same thing. It doesn't. Once you grasp the differences between idleness, faithfulness, added fruitfulness, and idolatry, you'll be able to keep yourself from a load of unnecessary guilt.

God designed our lives so that our various assignments aren't independent of each other. Shipwreck in one area will often mean shipwreck in other areas. But if we're being faithful in all our assignments, we can be confident they will all work together in a beautiful virtuous cycle to increase our fruitfulness across the board. For example, at work you learn to help dissatisfied customers, while at church you work to preserve unity by answering questions and concerns of fellow members. The skills you build in one area help you in other areas. The fruit increases everywhere!

In fact, the idea of balance may not be the right way to think about this at all. The assignments God gives us aren't *really* in competition with one another. They can't be, because they are all given by an infinitely wise God. All our assignments are really just parts of the one primary responsibility we have to follow and honor Jesus. Keep that in mind, and you will be able to avoid both idleness and idolatry. You will also press forward in fruitfulness as the Lord gives you the ability to do so. Most importantly, it will be to the glory of the One for whom you ultimately work, Jesus the King!

1. Read and Reflect: Matthew 6:25 – 34;
   2 Thessalonians 2:14; John 17:6; Ephesians 2:10;
   Ephesians 6:4; Hebrews 10:24 – 25; 1 Corinthians 3:5 – 9;
   1 Thessalonians 4:10 – 12; Ephesians 4:28; Proverbs 23:4

2. Think of an example in your life (or in the life of a
   friend) of the consequences of being called to some
   thing rather than being called to *Someone.* What fruit
   did that confusion bear?

3. Which good responsibilities has God given you
   (church, family, relationships, work, etc.) that you are
   most tempted to prioritize over him? How can Christian friends help you counter this tendency?

4. Do you have realistic expectations about what it looks
   like to be faithful in your relationships with family,
   church members, and colleagues? Find a Christian
   friend this week to discuss this with. Ask each other
   tough questions about these relationships.

5. Jesus has first called you to himself to be a disciple.
   Have you allowed otherwise good responsibilities to
   distract you from spending time with him? Has this
   impacted your spiritual growth?

6. How is aiming for faithfulness and fruitfulness different
   from pursuing balance?

CHAPTER 7

HOW DO I HANDLE DIFFICULT BOSSES AND COWORKERS?

Do you like your boss? How about your coworkers? The hardest thing about our jobs can be the people with whom we're expected to work. It's not as if those are insignificant relationships. Working with people who are uncaring, unfair, unreasonable, cutthroat, or incompetent can easily make a typical week painful and frustrating.

But let's be honest. The difficulty we perceive with our coworkers or bosses or employees often doesn't have as much to do with them as it does with us. If we've been harping on anything in this book, it's that we all have a tendency to think about our jobs in sinful and selfish ways—a tendency that extends not just to the tasks we perform but also to the people with whom we work.

If you make work an idol, you will perceive your boss as an obstacle and your coworkers as competitors. The way you perceive and treat your coworkers depends on whether they are smoothing the way toward your goal. Your boss? He has your job. Your coworker? He wants your job. And if you become idle in your job, you'll treat your boss with contempt and your coworkers will become sounding boards for your complaints.

The picture we're drawing here is probably a little stark on both sides. Our sins don't always make themselves quite so identifiable. However, if we're honest with ourselves, our description here may accurately reflect the bitter fruit of any idolatry or idleness that lives in our hearts. Ungodly thoughts about work lead to ungodly thoughts about our coworkers.

The biblical worldview we've been talking about in this book challenges and confronts our sinful attitudes toward our coworkers. It teaches us to think of them not as obstacles or competitors but as *people*—people made in God's image and loved by him. In short, it frees us to love our neighbors as we love ourselves in a place where love is often in radically short supply—the workplace.

FAITH-FUELED SERVICE

We've talked mostly about how the gospel changes the way we think about the actual work we do at our jobs. But the gospel also flips the way we think about the people with whom we work. Once you realize you work for Jesus and your first responsibility is to follow him, then you realize your job isn't just about you anymore. Your job becomes an arena in which to worship and bring honor to God. And guess what? The second most important way you do that—right after loving God—is by loving other people, according to Jesus.

Let's look again at that familiar passage in Colossians through a slightly wider lens. Paul writes these words in Colossians 3:22–4:1:

> Slaves, obey your earthly masters in everything; and do it, not only when their eye is on you and to curry their favor, but with sincerity of heart and reverence for the Lord. Whatever you do, work at it with all your heart, as working for the Lord, not for human masters, since you know that you will receive

an inheritance from the Lord as a reward. It is the Lord Christ you are serving. Anyone who does wrong will be repaid for their wrongs, and there is no favoritism.

Masters, provide your slaves with what is right and fair, because you know that you also have a Master in heaven.

How does this passage shed light on our relationships with our coworkers? Paul talks about slaves and masters, not employees and employers, but the principles that underlie the application of his message are the same. The way you treat other people should be colored by a vivid realization that God is watching!

Because we are applying this passage, which talks about slavery, to our relationships in the workplace today, we should pause for a moment and acknowledge that it's somewhat uncomfortable when we come to places in the New Testament that seem to take slavery as a given instead of calling for its immediate overthrow. That discomfort has led many people to point out that Roman slavery was very different from the slavery in the British Empire and the United States. There is some truth to that claim. There are important historical differences between these slaveries. Still, though, the fact remains that Roman slavery was not just a normal, everyday employer-employee relationship. It was an unjust system of forced labor, often cruel and sometimes lethal.

We may wonder why the writers of the New Testament seem to accept the existence of slavery. We could say much about this, and many books have been written on the subject. One reason is that the aim of Jesus and the apostles was simply deeper than the reformation of a social system. They were focused on the root of the problem—the sinful state of the human heart. The fact is that the unjust system wasn't the root of the sin of slavery, and simply changing the system wouldn't have solved the problem in any long-term sense. The sinful human heart would just find another way to oppress others, even if the system of

Roman slavery had been eliminated. So that's what Jesus and the apostles take aim at — the human heart, whatever system it finds itself under.

So when Paul or the other New Testament writers talk about slavery, we acknowledge they are speaking about a system that is somewhat removed from our current employee-employer relationships in the workplace. But the principles they advocate remain important because they are applying the truth of the gospel to the root cause — the sinful condition of our hearts. We all have relationships in which we are called to serve someone else. And we all need to be challenged, because our hearts will inevitably rebel against this.

In this passage, Paul challenges us to think about our responsibility as Christians *to serve those who are in authority over us*. If you are an employee, then even though the context is different from the system of Roman slavery, most of what Paul says to slaves is immediately applicable to you. One of the ways you are called to honor Jesus is to give yourself for the good of others. Your boss is one of those others. Paul urges us to obey those who are in authority over us "in everything." While that command certainly doesn't include sinful things, it *does* include stupid things. Your boss may give you tasks that are asinine in your opinion, but unless what he asks you to do is sinful, you should do it. Moreover, you should do it "with sincerity of heart and reverence for the Lord." That's what will honor Jesus.

Also, your obedience should really have nothing to do with whether your boss is watching you or not. Why? Because far more important than whether your boss's eye is on you is the inescapable fact that *God is watching you!* Always. Whatever you do, you should do it sincerely and with your whole heart, knowing that God sees. His eyes should provide more motivation for you than a quarterly performance review ever would.

Paul brings this same principle to bear on those who are in

authority over others. Just as an employee should remember that God is watching him or her, so should an employer. Paul writes, "Masters, provide your slaves with what is right and fair, because you know that you also have a Master in heaven." This is about more than just fair payment, though; it's about fair *treatment*. If you treat your employees with disrespect and unkindness, you can be sure your Master in heaven sees that. If you treat them with kindness, gentleness, love, and patience, you can be sure he sees that too.

A gospel-centered perspective on our work changes the way we think about our boss, as well as the way we think of our coworkers. We work ultimately for Jesus and should see our primary responsibility in our jobs as one of faith-fueled service. We work to love Jesus, and we work to serve others. Even if our bosses are difficult and our coworkers are mean, we are called to serve them because that brings honor to our King.

So what does it mean to be a faith-fueled servant in the workplace? We can identify several marks of a worker whose service is defined by faith in God and the good news of the gospel.

Mark #1: Determination Not to Complain

It is a rare and powerful witness *not* to complain at work. Complaints tend to be the common coin of the realm of the workplace. So when someone comes along who doesn't speak Complaint as their native language, the effect can be astonishing. Look at what Paul writes in Philippians 2:14–16:

> Do everything without grumbling or arguing, so that you may become blameless and pure, "children of God without fault in a warped and crooked generation." Then you will shine among them like stars in the sky as you hold firmly to the word of life.

Look carefully where this all starts—with the exhortation to "do everything without grumbling or arguing." Pretty unremarkable, right? But now look where it ends up. If you refrain from complaining or quarreling, you will "shine like stars in the sky"! You'll "hold firmly to the word of life"! Those are some astonishingly grand outcomes for doing something as simple-sounding as not complaining.

None of this is to say that holding back your complaints is easy. It's not! It's incredibly hard. We naturally want to let others know when our own circumstances are uniquely bad and therefore especially worthy of complaint. But faith-fueled service in the workplace means we will be marked by a spirit of dogged determination *not* to grumble, not to complain.

Mark #2: Happy Submission to Authority

If the first mark had to do with keeping a rein on our tongues, this one goes to the heart. As long as our bosses aren't asking us to sin, we should obey those in authority over us "with sincerity of heart" (Colossians 3:22), not with a plastic smile and a heart exploding with rage.

It is easy to submit when your boss is a paragon of kindness, respect, and goodwill. But when your boss is a flat-out jerk who is arrogant and self-absorbed, how you respond reveals your heart—whether you really are working for Jesus.

A friend of ours once worked for a boss who was absolutely brilliant in his profession. But he was also greedy, abrasive, and verbally abusive to his employees. He screamed at his employees regularly for the smallest infractions. It would have been easy for our friend to launch a war of attrition against this guy—to bad-mouth him in front of his peers, sabotage his projects, and even pass on sensitive information to rival companies. Instead, he decided to take a different angle because of his Christian convictions. Rather than fighting back, he decided to "obey ... with sincerity of heart" (Colossians 3:22) in the recognition that it was Jesus who had deployed him to this job at this time in his life, and therefore he could "work at it with all [his] heart, as working for the Lord, not for [a jerk]" (Colossians 3:23). He worked hard to make sure he spoke well of his boss to outsiders. He protected his boss's reputation, carefully guarded company secrets, and always tried to show the utmost respect to his boss. He prayed for the man to repent of his sin and to trust in Jesus for salvation.

Sadly, this story doesn't have a nice, happy ending. The man wasn't converted, and there was no dramatic turnaround. Our friend isn't even sure his boss noticed his behavior. But the point isn't whether the boss noticed; it's the fact that *God* noticed. For whatever reason, God had chosen to place our friend in that job for that season of his life. And our friend sought to honor the King as long as the King saw fit to have him there. He didn't act this way because the boss was worthy of his good service. Far from it! But Jesus the King *was* worthy—infinitely so. Service to Christ, therefore, meant service to the jerk. "Slaves, obey your earthly masters in everything; and do it, not only when their eye is on you and to curry their favor, but with sincerity of heart and reverence for the Lord" (Colossians 3:22).

If you're struggling with a difficult situation with a boss or coworker, try this. Start praying for that person every day. Pray for their family, their relationships, their circumstances, and their challenges. Pray for their salvation. Pray, too, that you would be able to work for them (or with them), not just with resignation, but with sincerity of heart.

Faith-fueled service in the workplace means we will be marked by happy submission to authority, even when it is not fun and even when it's not fair.

Mark #3: Unfeigned Humility

More than a few of our problems at work stem from feeling that something we've been asked to do is beneath us. "I shouldn't be asked to do that," we think. "I'm so much more valuable than that!" Really? What place does that kind of thinking have in a Christian's life? After all, if we are followers of Jesus, don't we have to expect that we will find ourselves doing a lot of things that aren't exactly commensurate with our "status"? Isn't that what Jesus himself did? Think about how Paul describes Jesus' work in Philippians 2:5–8:

> In your relationships with one another, have the same mindset as Christ Jesus:
>
> Who, being in very nature God,
> did not consider equality with God something to be
> used to his own advantage;
> rather, he made himself nothing
> by taking the very nature of a servant,
> being made in human likeness.
> And being found in appearance as a man,
> he humbled himself
> by becoming obedient to death—
> even death on a cross!

No matter how important you think you are and no matter how lowly the task you've been asked to do, you have *never*— never, never, never—stooped as low as Jesus stooped to save you. The Bible teaches emphatically that followers of Jesus should be people marked by conspicuous humility. They should not think too highly of themselves. They should consider others more important than themselves. They should have the same mind in themselves that was in Christ Jesus. Though he was God, he took the nature of a servant and became obedient even to death.

Once you take up the cross to follow Jesus, status just doesn't hold the value it once did. When once you find your worth in Christ's work and your identity in him, you realize you are free to serve in whatever role and capacity he may have for you. You can be confident he knows exactly what he's doing with your time and talents. In the end, it simply can't be beneath you if it comes from the hand of the King.

Faith-fueled service in the workplace means we will be marked by unfeigned humility that leads us to follow in the self-emptying footsteps of our King.

Mark #4: Godly Competitiveness

Another perennial problem in the workplace comes from clashing ambitions. We want the same thing somebody else wants, and this forces us into a cutthroat competition with our coworkers, suspicion of our employees, and even envy of our bosses. It's ambition run amok.

As Christians, the gospel frees us from the need to compete in ungodly ways with our peers. It rearranges and resets our ambitions. Instead of being driven merely to make much of ourselves, we're driven to make much of Jesus in everything we do.

Does this mean we should never compete against others? Let's be clear upfront. Competition is not a bad thing. Being a Christian doesn't mean we just have to curtsy and make way for everyone to pass us up. It's not competition the Bible forbids, but rather the *world's playbook* for competition — the cutthroat mentality that says the only way for you to go up is for everybody else to go down. Our goal as Christians is to compete with and love our coworkers all at the same time. How do we do that? We compete by working at whatever we do with all our heart, not by undercutting and sabotaging the efforts of our coworkers. *Compete*, but compete with honor. Win by running faster, not by tripping all your competitors. Even more, encourage them to run faster too. Help them see where they can improve their work, and congratulate them when they advance.

Faith-fueled service means having a spirit of godly competitiveness, working hard before the Lord rather than taking others down.

CONCLUSION

As with so many of the things we discuss in this book, there aren't any magic formulas for dealing with difficult bosses and coworkers. But sometimes a change of perspective can lead to a change of heart, which changes everything. If you've been thinking of your boss as an obstacle to your career advancement, pray and ask God to help you see that person as someone God wants you to serve. Then go do it. Work willingly, not grudgingly. Stop complaining and rolling your eyes. Be humble. Encourage.

Similarly, if you've been clashing with your coworkers, pray and ask God to help you see you've been called to serve them. Then, again, go and do it. Work hard. Offer to take tasks off their hands. Happily do tasks nobody really wants to do, and don't be a martyr about it. Love them, encourage them, and serve them, not because they deserve it from you, but because you didn't deserve it from Jesus either!

Our workplaces can be gloriously sanctifying places for us. Conflict, difficult authority figures, and competitive coworkers are just some of the things God uses to mold and shape us into the Jesus-reflecting people he wants us to be. Don't resent it if he's put those things in your life right now. Figure out how he wants you to respond to them in order to become more like Jesus. Remember, you are in your job not just to pay the bills and not just to advance your career. You're there to serve Jesus. Learn to serve and love others — whether they deserve it or not.

1. Read and Reflect: Colossians 3:22 – 4:1;
   Philippians 2:5 – 8, 14 – 16

2. Because we are sinful, it doesn't come natural to not
   complain or to happily submit or to be truly humble.
   Which mark listed in this chapter do you find the most
   difficult? Why? Pray that God will change your heart to
   be faithful and honor him through your work.

3. What does Jesus' submission to sinful, imperfect
   earthly authorities teach us about our own submission
   to imperfect bosses, managers, and directors at work?

4. Who at your workplace is the hardest for you to love?
   Do you ever pray for them? Do they know you are a
   Christian? Do you excuse yourself from loving them?

5. What are some practical ways that you can love and
   serve your boss or coworkers this week?

6. Do you work with any Christians? If so, consider meeting with them to strategize about how to encourage
   one another and be a bright witness for God in your
   workplace.

CHAPTER 8

WHAT DOES IT MEAN TO BE A CHRISTIAN BOSS?

The topic of leadership has attracted more attention from the world than any other subject we'll talk about in this book. A search on Amazon for books on leadership yields 86,000 results. In all likelihood, some of those books will be genuinely good ones. God hasn't reserved all the wise answers and helpful advice on this topic for Christians. A number of authors who write and speak about leadership are saying some genuinely good and useful things: *Be humble and charismatic. Cast vision. Inspire followers, create motivation, align goals, build teams. Persevere against daunting odds. Be morally grounded.* All of this is good advice!

One of our favorite writers on the subject of leadership is Jim Collins, author of *Good to Great*. The main difference he notices between a good company and a great one is the person who leads it. Leaders of great companies lead through a paradoxical blend of personal humility and professional will. They have a profound commitment to seeing the company succeed, but that commitment is unrelated to their own personal legacy or burgeoning bank account. As Christians, we can both affirm and aspire to that definition of a leader. It seems like a really good one, in fact! So what is different about the picture of leadership we get from the Bible?

As Christians, we understand that the authority we hold over others is not inherent to us. It's not derived from our boss or our corporation, nor does it come from the bare fact that their livelihood is dependent on us in some way. No, whatever authority we have is derived from God. Hence, we have an obligation to exercise our authority, not just for the good of the company, but also for the good of those over whom we have authority. No matter how high we are in our organization, any authority we hold over other people is given to us by God. "Love your neighbor as yourself" is operative even in the boss's chair.

We can easily find ourselves falling into idolatry and idleness when it comes to authority. If you make an idol of your work, you will ultimately end up *using* your employees. Far from loving them and caring for them as people, you'll conscript them into your mission to find ultimate satisfaction in your own accomplishments. They'll become little more than foot soldiers in your breakneck pursuit of your god. Conversely, if you become idle in your work, you'll ultimately wind up neglecting and demoralizing those you lead. You'll be listless and disengaged. Instead of helping your employees see God's purposes in their own work, you'll end up communicating that neither you nor God cares much at all about what they are doing.

PRINCIPLES OF AUTHORITY

That is *not* how we want to lead our employees! After all, King Jesus has deployed us in this season of our lives to lead. Therefore, we should do it in a way that will honor him — which means caring for and loving our employees. We must teach them about God's own authority and his purposes for them in their work. This is only possible when we have a deep understanding of what authority is, where it comes from, and how it can be used in a godly way. Let's think about it in terms of six principles of authority taught in the Bible.

Principle #1: Authority Is from God

It all comes from God. God created human beings and assigned them the task of ruling over and subduing the earth. Genesis 1:28 reads, "God blessed them and said to them, 'Be fruitful and increase in number; fill the earth and subdue it. Rule over the fish in the sea and the birds in the sky and over every living creature that moves on the ground.'" Humanity's perch at the top of the created order wasn't just a matter of raw strength or intelligence; it was a divine grant of authority. Adam and Eve were to exercise that authority in the way God wanted it exercised. They were to cultivate the garden, not destroy it. They were to name the animals and rule them, not cruelly dominate them.

The same is true for any authority God has given to you. It is not yours by right; it is a divine grant. Therefore, you are to wield that authority for the good of those over whom you wield it, not just for your own purposes. It is really just a matter of faithful obedience to the King, but it also communicates to the world around you about what your King is like. When you use authority well, you show your employees and everyone around you that authority is ultimately a good thing, that it comes from a God who himself exercises authority with perfect love and perfect justice. How you wield authority, therefore, really says more about the God you serve than it does about you.

Principle #2: Authority Should Serve and Bless Others

The Bible repeatedly teaches that the wise exercise of authority leads to blessing for those who are under it. Joseph's authority in

Egypt enabled that nation to weather seven years of withering famine. Nehemiah used his authority among the returning exiles of Jerusalem to complete the wall that would defend them from their enemies. Even the last recorded words of King David in 2 Samuel 23:3–4 are a plea for kings after him to exercise royal authority rightly:

> When one rules over people in righteousness,
>   when he rules in the fear of God,
> he is like the light of morning at sunrise
>   on a cloudless morning,
> like the brightness after rain
>   that brings grass from the earth.

We're going to guess you're neither the vice-regent of Pharaoh nor a king, but the principle is the same for you: authority rightly exercised leads to flourishing. When you use authority to build up and not tear down, to right wrongs and not perpetrate them, to encourage and not crush, to work for others' good and not just for your own, the result will be light and life in your workplace. Read David's words again: "When one [manages employees] in righteousness, when he [leads his company] in the fear of God, he is like the light of morning at sunrise on a cloudless morning." There just aren't many bosses like that in the world. Followers of King Jesus, though, should be some of them.

Principle #3: Authority Can Be Terribly Abused

Most people in the world around us think of authority as a bad and fearsome thing, something to be avoided if at all possible. Sufficient evidence exists to prove that where there is authority, it will most likely be abused. But this is not how God intended it from the beginning. When Adam and Eve sinned, the world fell, and authority went with it. So now, we human beings—all of us—are by nature selfish sinners. Everything, including the authority we exercise, becomes a tool for building ourselves up and tearing others down. Jesus understood this. "You know," he said, "that the rulers of the Gentiles lord it over them, and their high officials exercise authority over them" (Matthew 20:25). That's how most of us think about authority. We assume that those who are in authority will use it to dominate us, oppress us, and even abuse us. Sadly, in a world of sin, that is far too often the case.

But then look at what Jesus says right after that: "Not so with you" (Matthew 20:26). We should recognize and reject the world's sinful abuse of authority and determine to use it for good, as God intended. This requires constant vigilance. Keep a watch over your heart. Make sure you aren't slipping into the world's patterns of lording it over your employees and using them for your own purposes. Don't use for evil and selfish purposes what God intended as a source of light and life for others.

Principle #4: Authority Should Imitate Jesus

Because we follow Jesus as King, we should strive to use authority like he does. It's like Paul writes in Philippians 2:5, "Have the same mindset as Christ Jesus." What does that mean? It means you should "in humility value others above yourselves, not looking to your own interests but each of you to the interests of the others" (Philippians 2:3–4). After all, that's what Jesus did. He humbled himself for our sake—even to death on the cross.

If the King of the universe humbled himself to death and looked to your interests rather than to his own, how could you ever think anything less would be sufficient for you? Use the authority God has given you in the same way that King Jesus uses his.

Principle #5: Authority Should Be Sacrificial

Jesus used his kingly authority for our eternal good. We see the same principle in his teaching about authority. After telling his disciples what authority is not (that is, lording it over people), he tells them in Matthew 20:26–28 what leadership ought to be:

> "Instead, whoever wants to become great among you must be your servant, and whoever wants to be first must be your slave—just as the Son of Man did not come to be served, but to serve, and to give his life as a ransom for many."

Godly leaders serve others. They look out for them and work for their good. Service is always costly. It'll cost you your priorities for the day at times. It'll cost you your limited time. It might even cost you some of your company's profits. But this is what Jesus calls us to do with the authority he gives us—to give ourselves for the good of others.

Principle #6: Godly Use of Authority Is Gospel Motivated and Grace Empowered

We hope you've picked up on this truth pretty clearly as you've read this chapter. The only way we'll ever know how to exercise authority rightly is by taking our cues from our King. Because he humbled himself for our sake, we are freed from a conception of authority that knows only how to lord it over others. Our identity and reward are not finally tied to our job performance but are found in Christ. We are freed from an exercise of authority that knows only how to use people and drive them like pack animals toward a goal. The gospel empowers us to make much of Christ by loving, serving, and blessing others.

That doesn't mean we decide somehow that accomplishments don't matter. It doesn't mean we can't spur one another on toward team goals and even correct and reprimand employees and coworkers when they're not doing the job. But it does mean that when we spur our employees on and even when we correct them, we do so, not with thoughts of our own glory and reputation, but with graciousness and a genuine, loving concern for their good and the good of the team.

GETTING PRACTICAL: HOW CAN YOU LEAD AND MANAGE WELL?

The most important strategy for leading well is to cultivate a heart that really desires to do so. There's no substitute for *want*. If you ultimately don't care how you lead, then no set of tactics and tips can ever make you a good and godly leader. Once you've cultivated a genuine desire to lead as Jesus would lead, it's important to think about what that will mean tomorrow at work. What will you do differently? What will you never do again? We can't give you all the answers to those questions. You'll have to do a lot of that thinking on your own, bringing to bear on your own situation the principles discussed here. But perhaps we can prime the pump with a few ideas that arise out of our own attempts to use authority well.

A very easy and revolutionary idea is to pray for those who work for you. That's one of the best things I (Seb) have ever done for the people who work for me. I pray—whether they are Christians or not—that they will find their work a joy, that it won't be burdensome to them, and that they will find contentment in it. I pray also for their families and even for specific things I know are going on in their families' lives. I also pray for my own interactions with them, for areas of potential conflict that might arise. I confess if I've spoken harshly, selfishly, or condescendingly to them and ask God to give me a heart that will respond selflessly and graciously. And I even pray for opportunities to share the gospel with them. Is there any better way to love your employees than by praying to the King specifically for them?

I've also found it incredibly helpful to schedule regular one-on-one meetings with my employees. It's a bit like discipling them, not only (or sometimes not even at all) as Christians, but as workers and people. Several years ago, I started trying to spend thirty minutes a week with each person I manage. I give them fifteen minutes to talk about anything on their minds, from work to family, and then I take fifteen minutes to talk with them about things on my mind—normally their work and priorities. I also try to give them godly encouragement and criticism when necessary, all with the intent of building them up as workers and people. Yes, this takes time, but you will soon begin to see the fruit of this investment of time in the lives of the people you meet with.

You can develop a mentoring relationship with one or more of your employees. Far too few bosses in the world are willing to give the time and effort it takes to serve as mentors to those coming behind them. Young workers are starving for career counseling and wisdom from older, more experienced Christians who can help them see how the gospel should impact their work lives. Serving younger workers in that way doesn't have to be a lifetime commitment. Agree to meet a few times and then make a decision about whether to continue meeting together. Mentoring someone in a deep way is a powerful opportunity, not only to train and prepare that person for greater responsibility, but also to model a culture of generosity that can eventually affect your entire organization.

CONCLUSION

I'll admit it. Managing people has been a struggle for me (Seb) over the years. I saw my employees merely as a means to my own ends, and I managed them like a sledgehammer manages a rock—they were in my way and needed to get out of it as quickly as possible! Needless to say, that mentality didn't lend itself very well to displaying God's good authority to them.

Over the years, by God's grace, I've seen some slow but steady growth in this area of my life, but it's still an area of constant struggle. What about you? Do you strive to use your authority to build others up in your workplace? Do you remind yourself every day that whatever authority you hold comes from the hand of your King? Do you therefore seek to exercise that authority as he would exercise it? Or does none of that ever really cross your mind?

Remember that even if you're the boss, you are one who works for Jesus. Recommit yourself to exercising your God-given authority in such a way that your King will be honored and revered, even among those with whom you work.

1. Read and Reflect: Genesis 1:28; 2 Samuel 23:3 – 4; Matthew 20:25 – 28

2. Think about those people you exercise authority over, formally or informally. It may be an employee or an intern. How did your life this past week faithfully model — or muddle — godly authority and commend the gospel to them?

3. The biblical view of authority is countercultural and radically different from the world's perspective. What do you think are the most important differences?

4. Have you been given, or do you desire, more responsibility and authority in your work? List three or four specific ways you can glorify God through a biblical approach to authority in your own context.

5. Are you a boss or worker who only cares about colleagues for their output? Think about people who may report to you or look up to you, and list one way you can pray for each of them this week.

6. Have you ever apologized to someone in your workplace for your attitude, speech, or actions toward them? What was it for? Do you need to do so now?

CHAPTER 9

HOW CAN I SHARE THE GOSPEL AT WORK?

One of our good friends, Hunter, was used by God to share the gospel with a coworker named Ashok, and by God's grace, Ashok came to faith in Jesus. Ashok is now a faithful member of a church, growing as a Christian and striving to do his own work in the name of King Jesus. We asked Ashok to share with us how he came to realize that the gospel of Jesus was true and that he needed to believe in it. Here's a portion of what he said to us:

> I don't remember when I met Hunter, but I think it was after a sales call that I just said to him, "So you're a Christian, right?" He answered me, and after that I just remember being friends with him. I liked Hunter. He was interesting, funny, really good at his job, and seemed to have depth as a person. We talked about all sorts of stuff—Lord of the Rings, *The Simpsons*, *Seinfeld*, work stuff, family stuff. But there was also something about Hunter that I knew I didn't really get. At some point he asked me if I'd be interested in reading and talking through the book of Mark with him. "The chapters are really short," he told me, "so we could chat about one or

two chapters for a few minutes and then just hang out like we always do." For reasons only the Holy Spirit can explain, I said, "Sure, why not?"

I had never encountered Jesus Christ before, but reading through that book I found him so attractive. He seemed so real. His words were warm—and haunting too. Hunter answered my questions and explained at times what was really going on. He explained sin too, telling me we are all sinners and describing where we go when we die if we haven't repented and put our faith in Christ. Hunter also spent some capital stored up in our friendship to invite me to church. I went, and the people I met after the service were so much more normal than I expected! I started visiting the church regularly. I was attracted to hearing God's Word. It shined a light into my dark life, bringing me very low before lifting me up. God saved me in August 2002.

What an incredible story! And yet—come on, is it really always that easy to share your faith? How often has someone turned to you at work and said, "So you're a Christian, right?" If only that would happen every week, workplace evangelism would be a piece of cake!

Sadly, stories like Ashok's are not a common occurrence. We can be as kind, gentle, loving, caring, humble, patient, good, and downright wonderful as we want. And still our coworkers will likely assume we just especially enjoyed our bagel that morning. There's an old saying often attributed to Saint Francis: "Preach the gospel always. If necessary, use words." That sounds nice, but it's nonsense. You have to use words if you want to preach the gospel. After all, it's good *news*. And sharing news requires words! It's rare for people to follow the Sunday school script of walking up to someone and saying, "You know, you're such a good person. What makes you different? Please share the gospel of Jesus with me." If the people around you are ever going to know the gospel message, they're not just going to learn it from your life-well-lived; you're going to have to tell them.

IDOLATRY, IDLENESS, AND EVANGELISM

Of course, sharing the gospel is another area that is deeply affected by our idolatry or idleness in our work. If you have made your job an idol, then likely you may not be especially sensitive to opportunities to speak the gospel to your coworkers. On the contrary, the pursuit of fame, prestige, money, and advancement probably dwarfs every other consideration in your mind, and there's no way you're going to jeopardize a promotion by talking about the gospel to the guy who's going to make the decision. Similarly, why talk about *spiritual* things to your employees when there are much more important *business* concerns to hash out with them? Idolatry of work will blind you. It will keep your eyes from seeing the spiritual realities around you.

But idleness in your work is poisonous for evangelism too. It's hard to do your work with joy when work seems purposeless. You'll complain and grumble, sigh and whine, and generally make yourself a magnet for disaffection and disillusion. Even if people are attracted to your cynicism, it still isn't an avenue for the gospel. If you've already marked yourself as someone characterized by idleness, cynicism, and general disengagement in the daily grind, it doesn't matter how much passion you feel when you say, "And so now I do *everything* I do for Jesus' glory!" They're just not going to listen to you. It's as simple as that. Idleness in your work will destroy your credibility to talk about the gospel of Jesus.

Once you repent of idolatry and idleness, though, your eyes are open to spiritual realities, and you become the kind of person who is living a life that adorns the gospel you speak. The Bible tells us that part of what it means to be followers of Christ is that we are nothing less than his representatives. Look at how Paul puts it in 2 Corinthians 5:17, 19 – 20:

> If anyone is in Christ, the new creation has come: The old has gone, the new is here!... And [God] has committed to us the message of reconciliation. We are therefore Christ's ambassadors, as though God were making his appeal through us.

Did you ever think about that? As a Christian, you are a fully credentialed, decked-out ambassador of the empire of Jesus the Christ, High King of the universe. God has committed to you the message of reconciliation, the message of the good news that Jesus reconciles sinners to God. And guess what? That's as true from 9:00 a.m. to 5:00 p.m. Monday through Friday as it is for any other hour of your life. When you go to church, you are an ambassador for the King. When you hang out with friends, you are an ambassador for the King. When you go to work, meet with a client, participate in a meeting, work on a project, drive a nail, create a blueprint, welcome a customer, or write a white paper, you are still an ambassador for the King. Evangelism isn't the primary purpose for our work. The Bible reveals to us all kinds of purposes and motivations for our work. However, we shouldn't kid ourselves. One of the purposes is evangelism. We are ambassadors for the King always, including the time we are at our jobs.

So how can we faithfully share the gospel with people at work?

1. Just do good work as a Christian. When you get a chance to speak the gospel to one of your coworkers, make sure you've already been backing it up by being a good and faithful worker yourself. Build a reputation as a person who works with purpose, creativity, kindness, and encouragement. Then when you get to share the gospel, people will see reflections in you of the character of your great King.

Practically, you can hold up your challenges at work to the light of the gospel and ask yourself how you can approach them "as working for the Lord" (Colossians 3:23). Would Jesus have you cut corners on that project? Would he have you defraud that client by doing that job on the cheap? Would he have you rip into your employees when they make mistakes, even stupid ones? Would he have you mope through your day in a spirit of resentment and anger? No. He would have you confront your challenges with faith that, ultimately, they are all coming from his hand. In the midst of it all, he would have you "shine among them like stars in the sky as you hold firmly to the word of life" (Philippians 2:16). Then the gospel you speak will be confirmed in the eyes of those who are watching you.

2. Learn to put God on the table. Yep, just throw him out there! Let people know in natural, easygoing, confident ways that you are a Christian. Why do so many Christians try to keep their Christianity a secret? We all want somebody to come to us and ask about Christianity (because that saves us the awkward experience of having to start that conversation ourselves), but often we go out of our way not to give them any opportunity to do so.

When somebody asks you what you did over the weekend, for crying out loud, tell them you went to church! Mention the Bible study you attend on Tuesday nights. Don't just mumble, "I'm sorry I can't come to your birthday party; I'm busy." Say, "I can't come because I'm scheduled to work at my church's clothes closet this weekend." You don't have to be obnoxious or irresponsible about it. Just make sure you identify yourself very publicly with Jesus. Let people know somehow that you're a Christian, and don't mentally censor your Christianity out of your interactions and conversations. You'll be amazed at how often people will take the opportunity to press in on the little piece of information you've just given them. People are often more interested in spiritual things than you think. They just need a little bit of permission from you to feel free to talk about them.

3. Build relationships beyond the office. Strive to break through the personal/professional boundaries that can form between you and your coworkers. Of course, you shouldn't let your relationships become inappropriate in any way. However, if you are going to share the gospel with someone, you will eventually have to talk to them about something other than the job.

Really, it's not too terribly difficult to do. Grab a cup of coffee after work. Ask questions that go beyond the usual shallow chitchat that often marks offices. Give some information about yourself that encourages the other person to open up as well. Talk about your family. Be honest about some of the struggles in your life, or talk about some of your hopes for the future. In time, by your questions, your openness, and your interest in their life, you'll communicate that you care about them far more deeply than just the talents they contribute to the company. You care about them *for them*. They'll be far more likely to listen to you talk about the gospel if they know they're not just another cog in your professional machine.

4. Use the witness of the church. As you build relationships with people, look for ways to involve other Christians from your church as well. One of the greatest witnesses to the gospel on the planet is the love that Christians have for one another. If you and some friends from church are going to be hanging out together, invite one of your coworkers to come along. The conversation doesn't have to be explicitly spiritual. Sometimes, interactions between a group of normal, interesting, fun, intelligent Christians will change a person's entire perspective about Christianity. Also, invite coworkers to your church's worship services. Let them see what it's like for a group of Christians to gather and take their faith seriously. Many non-Christians have never seen anything like that, and experiencing it can raise all kinds of good questions in their minds. Jesus called his followers to gather together into churches for a reason. Your church family can be an enormous evangelistic resource. Let them be coworkers with you as you hold firmly to the word of life in your workplace.

5. Have a "mission field" mind-set about your work. Have you ever considered that one of the reasons God may have deployed you to your job is so you can help break into a particular subculture with the message of the gospel? Throughout our society, there are countless groups of people who share much in common simply because they work in the same field. They speak the same jargon; they struggle with the same issues; they ask many of the same questions. And sadly, in many of those subcultures, the truth of the gospel is a rare thing indeed. For example, I imagine I (Seb) am one of only a tiny number of Christians working in the creative internet space today. That means I have the privilege of helping to break into that subculture with the message of the gospel. What specific group of people has the King deployed you to work among each day? Architects? Teachers? Auto salespeople? Thinking about it that way helps us to not get discouraged by the thought of millions of people who need to hear the gospel. Rather, we are energized by the thought that we've been deployed by our King to a specific network of friends and relationships into which we can speak truth that has seldom been heard.

You could also consider taking your job to another part of the world, even places where it may be difficult for career missionaries to go. The globalization of the business world is one of the most important developments in missions in all of history. Companies are expanding internationally and looking for professionals, experts, and entrepreneurs to open up new markets where none have existed. Why not consider being an engineer in Shanghai? Why not do your business in Dubai, Istanbul, or Moscow, where millions of people from hundreds of nationalities live and work every day? These places need a strong gospel witness. Career missionaries who are already in many of these cities will be deeply encouraged by other Christians moving to their cities and putting their hands to the plow.

BE WISE AND WINSOME, BUT NOT WORRIED AND WIMPY

Workplace evangelism gets a bad rap sometimes. People assume that when you do it, it's going to be tactless, awkward, and disruptive in some way. It doesn't have to be that way. You can do good work, make your faith known, talk to your coworkers about their lives, and invite them to meet other Christians—and it can be as natural as becoming friends. An ambassador of the kingdom of Jesus should be wise and winsome. She should look for opportunities to make it known that she's a follower of Jesus, but she doesn't need to be arrogant or obnoxious about it. She should take advantage of openings in conversations and be willing to defend her faith when necessary, but do so in a way that attracts people rather than repelling them. Wise and winsome is worth pursuing.

Unfortunately, Christians often seem to equate "wisdom" in any given situation with "being quiet." "Oh, it wouldn't have been wise for me to speak up there," we say. Or "Oh, I don't think letting myself be known as a Christian would have been the wisest course there—too much potential for offense to be taken." And in time, we find ourselves being "wise" like that in our jobs for a decade—to the point that our coworkers would be shocked to find out we regularly attend church. An innocent bystander might mistake "wise and winsome" for little more than "worried and wimpy"!

They say the better part of courage is wisdom and discretion. That's true, but so is the reverse. The better part of wisdom and discretion is courage. If you're an ambassador of the King, you simply have to let that fact be known. You have to talk about it sometimes. Yes, it can lead to some awkward moments and weird conversations. Every ambassador deals with awkward moments and weird conversations. When you declare yourself to be a follower of King Jesus, you're making a declaration about King Jesus' claims over everybody in the room. Everybody knows that's what you're doing, so there's no getting around it. You're saying that King Jesus rose from the dead and that he saves sinners—and that *nobody else in the universe* does that. That's not exactly cocktail party banter. If your definition of *wise* and *winsome* is "only speaks about Jesus when there's no chance of offending anyone," you may as well hang it up. You won't find one of those.

Think about it. God may have deployed you in your particular job with all the potential for awkward conversations precisely because he *wants* you to handle it. So be wise and winsome, but don't morph into worried and wimpy. Speak about the King, even at work. After all, he's already promised to be with us to the very end of the age (Matthew 28:20).

1. Read and Reflect: 2 Corinthians 5:17–20; Philippians 2:16; Matthew 28:20

2. Have you shared the gospel with anyone in your workplace in the past year? Ever? What excuses do you use to prevent your faithfulness to God in this area? Who at your office would be surprised if they found out you are a Christian?

3. Are there other Christians at your workplace? How can you meet with them to pray for the office or to strategize on how to be a winsome witness for the gospel?

4. Making work an idol can lead some Christians to focus too much on the tasks at hand rather than on investing in others. However, being idle can lead some Christians to fail to honor God through their work and even to poorly reflect the gospel. Have you seen either of those negative examples in your workplace? How can you learn from this?

5. Is your reputation at work more important to you than being a faithful, winsome witness for Jesus? If so, repent and ask God to change your heart so you can find joy in serving Jesus the King.

6. How is your job a mission field? Pray that God will give you an increasing vision for how he can use your job for the Great Commission.

CHAPTER 10

IS FULL-TIME MINISTRY MORE VALUABLE THAN MY JOB?

M y (Seb's) first job out of college was with a consulting firm. It was great training for a career in business, and it paid enough too, but I found myself being discontented with what I was doing. Helping companies become more profitable just didn't seem meaningful to me. Over the years, I've held a number of other jobs, and the question of meaning popped up in every one of them. How was it not just a waste of my time to be helping banks merge some branches or helping a utility company price power? How could God ever be glorified by *this*?

This struggle to find meaning in our work is not unique. We have conversations regularly with people who are frustrated with their jobs because they can't see how what they do is a strategic, meaningful use of their time. They look at pastors and missionaries and think, "Now, *that's* meaningful work. Compared to that, designing a bridge to alleviate traffic problems in such-and-such a city is just valueless."

Is that true? Are there some jobs that are more valuable in God's eyes than others? Are there some jobs that are more meaningful than others? Are you wasting your time if you don't quit your "meaningless" job and start applying at missions agencies? We think the answer to those questions is no, and we want to show you why we think that's the case.

Ultimately, the struggle with thinking your job isn't valuable grows out of a mind-set of idleness about work. If you fail to see God's purposes in what you're doing, it's incredibly easy to look at where he's deployed someone else and think, "I'd rather be doing that." On the other hand, if you've made an idol of your work, this kind of question will infuriate you, and you'll respond to it very differently. Instead of feeling like *your* work is valueless, you'll work overtime to explain to yourself why *other people's* work is not as meaningful as your own.

We believe both those ways of thinking are wrong. In fact, we think the whole question is wrong, because the whole game of trying to assign relative value to this job or that one is ultimately a fruitless waste of time. The world is far too complicated and God is far too sovereign for that inherently selfish exercise to be of any use. Think about it. The whole big idea we've promoted in this book is that the value of our work isn't finally found at all in the particular thing we do; it's found in the fact that whatever we do, we do it for our King.

In a way, the whole conversation about which job is more valuable in God's sight is reminiscent of the disciples arguing about which one of them was greatest. Of course, they all had their cases to make. Peter would have pointed to the fact that he was the first to confess Jesus as the Christ. John would have said Jesus loved him best. Bartholomew would have come up with something too. But it didn't matter. The whole conversation was ridiculous and sinful, and Jesus rebuked them for it. And we believe he'd have a similar reaction to our conversations about whose job is greatest.

DO THE MATH

As large as this question looms in our minds sometimes, we should realize we're talking about a really small slice of our lives. For the vast majority of the hours in a week, God calls us to do exactly the same things, regardless of what we do for a job. Let's do the math.

Consider two guys—one a businessman and the other a pastor. Let's call one—oh, I don't know—Seb, and the other, Greg. They both have 168 hours in a week. They both get seven to eight hours of sleep a night. If both are pursuing biblical faithfulness in their assignments, then they're spending something like 65 percent of their waking lives doing exactly the same things! They'll be serving in their churches. They'll be loving their wives and raising their children. They'll be spending time with their friends and neighbors—solving problems and looking for opportunities to share the gospel with people they know. And then, in the remaining 35 percent of their lives, they'll both go to work and strive to labor faithfully for their King.

Do you see the point? When you consider the entirety of their lives, there's simply not much difference between what God has called Greg and Seb to do. Even in the hours in which God has deployed them to do different things, they have the same first responsibility—to follow Jesus and seek to honor him in all they do. Understanding that fact provides quite a lot of perspective. It approaches downright silliness to say one of them is living a life that is somehow more valuable in God's eyes than the other's life.

WHAT DOES GOD VALUE?

Still, though, what about the 35 percent? Can't we still have a discussion about whose 35 percent is more valuable in God's sight? Isn't it a given that God values the work of a pastor more than he does a businessperson or a police officer? Well, no. God deploys each of us to do what he would have us to do, and the Bible makes it very clear that determining what he values is far beyond our competence.

Examples are all over the place in the Bible. David was chosen to be king of Israel. Nobody thought David would be the one whom God would choose for the job. After all, David's brothers were older and taller and stronger — they were soldiers! — and everybody knew a soldier was more valuable in God's sight than a shepherd. Yet, when the time came for the king to be anointed, it was the shepherd whom God chose. Actually, the whole story of the nation of Israel underlines this point. Israel wasn't powerful or rich. She wasn't even really a nation — by any realistic definition of that word. In fact, if you would have had a conversation about which nation God might have valued most in the world, Israel would barely have made the list. Yet despite all that, God chose them and called them "his people, his treasured possession" (Deuteronomy 7:6) and "the apple of his eye" (Deuteronomy 32:10). Who could have guessed it would be a pathetic little nation like Israel that God would value above all others?

Jesus' parable of the workers in Matthew 20:1 – 16 makes the same point:

> "For the kingdom of heaven is like a landowner who went out early in the morning to hire workers for his vineyard. He agreed to pay them a denarius for the day and sent them into his vineyard.
>
> "About nine in the morning he went out and saw others standing in the marketplace doing nothing. He told them, 'You also go and work in my vineyard, and I will pay you whatever is right.' So they went.
>
> "He went out again about noon and about three in the afternoon and did the same thing. About five in the afternoon he went out and found still others standing around. He asked

them, 'Why have you been standing here all day long doing nothing?'

" 'Because no one has hired us,' they answered.

"He said to them, 'You also go and work in my vineyard.'

"When evening came, the owner of the vineyard said to his foreman, 'Call the workers and pay them their wages, beginning with the last ones hired and going on to the first.'

"The workers who were hired about five in the afternoon came and each received a denarius. So when those came who were hired first, they expected to receive more. But each one of them also received a denarius. When they received it, they began to grumble against the landowner. 'These who were hired last worked only one hour,' they said, 'and you have made them equal to us who have borne the burden of the work and the heat of the day.'

"But he answered one of them, 'I am not being unfair to you, friend. Didn't you agree to work for a denarius? Take your pay and go. I want to give the one who was hired last the same as I gave you. Don't I have the right to do what I want with my own money? Or are you envious because I am generous?'

"So the last will be first, and the first will be last."

The point of this incredible story is simple. We should never assume that God's standard of value and honor is the same as ours. The workers had a certain standard of value they expected to be operative. If an hour of work earned a denarius, then twelve hours ought to earn twelve. But the reality was that all the money was the Lord's, and he had the right to pay it out by his grace in any way he chose. He wasn't operating according to their standards of what was valuable work and what was not.

We, too, have all kinds of standards by which we try to determine the value of people and what they do. Sometimes our standard is success. Sometimes it's pure utilitarianism. Other times it's our perception of how spiritual a particular job is. If it's a job in the church, we think God must value it more than he values a job in an office building.

Can you see the folly of that kind of thinking in light of this parable? Our standards of what is valuable, of what deserves reward, are not necessarily God's standards at all! That's why the whole conversation about the relative value of our jobs is so wrongheaded. We should never fool ourselves into thinking that God always honors the things we honor, overlooks the things we overlook, or values the things we value. His standard is his own. His rewards are his own. He will give them to his people as he sees fit, and his judgment will be exactly right.

HEAD AND SHOULDERS, KNEES AND TOES

If value is not the right way to think about our jobs in relation to each other, what is? Well, consider what Paul writes in Romans 12:3–8 about the way Jesus distributes gifts in the local church:

> For by the grace given me I say to every one of you: Do not think of yourself more highly than you ought, but rather think of yourself with sober judgment, in accordance with the faith God has distributed to each of you. For just as each of us has one body with many members, and these members do not all have the same function, so in Christ we, though many, form one body, and each member belongs to all the others. We have different gifts, according to the grace given to each of us. If your gift is prophesying, then prophesy in accordance with your faith; if it is serving, then serve; if it is teaching, then teach; if it is to encourage, then give encouragement; if it is giving, then give generously; if it is to lead, do it diligently; if it is to show mercy, do it cheerfully.

Yes, this passage is speaking about the local church, but we believe the same principles hold when we apply them to society at large. The best way to think about our jobs in relation to one another is not to try to determine which have more value relative to others, but rather to realize they all work together as one harmonious whole, like a body. In 1 Corinthians 12:17–19, Paul writes these words:

> If the whole body were an eye, where would the sense of hearing be? If the whole body were an ear, where would the sense of smell be? But in fact God has placed the parts in the body, every one of them, just as he wanted them to be. If they were all one part, where would the body be? As it is, there are many parts, but one body.

How do you decide which part of the body is most valuable? Would you rather lose an eye or an ear, your brain or your heart? What if your thumbs rebelled and decided they were going to resign from being thumbs and apply to be ears?

You can see the point. Just as God didn't design the physical body to be just one part, so he didn't design the body of the church to be just one part either. And this principle can be applied to God's purposes in the wider world as well. God certainly intended to have some people serve as pastors and missionaries. But he also intended there would be police officers, teachers, carpenters, businesspeople, salespeople, inspectors, waiters, legislators, and all kinds of other "parts" that would function together to keep the larger "body" of human society functioning smoothly.

There are all kinds of lessons to be learned here. For starters, nobody who is working and making a contribution to the larger "body" of human society should ever fool themselves into thinking their contribution is not of value. As Paul writes about the church, "Those parts of the body that seem to be weaker are indispensable" (1 Corinthians 12:22). We all have our own ideas about which jobs are important and which are not as necessary. But often, the jobs we don't give a thought about prove to be more significant than we might think. Society, like the church, is an organic, interrelated matrix of relationships. The work that one person does affects the lives of others, no matter how small and insignificant that job may appear to be.

If you struggle with thinking your own job is worthless, perhaps you should think about what would happen if nobody did the job you do. How long, really, would the system last before it crashed? How would society as a whole be affected? Your job isn't indispensable — no job is — but it's probably not as dispensable as you might assume.

If you have the opposite problem and are convinced that your job is one of the most important in the world, pay attention to Paul's warning in 1 Corinthians 12:21: "The eye cannot say to the hand, 'I don't need you!' And the head cannot say to the feet, 'I don't need you!'" Think about it. What would you do if all those "less important" jobs around you disappeared? How well would your job continue to function? How well does the vaunted eye function without the rest of the body? How well does the head do when it doesn't have the other members of the body to support it? Not very well! The same is true of you. You can talk until you're blue in the face about how valuable your job is. Yet, the fact remains that your job is just one part of the whole array of jobs in the societal body that God has put together, and without the other parts, yours would cease to function.

The point, again, is that "value" is simply not the right question. Paul makes that very clear in his teachings in Romans 12 and 1 Corinthians 12. Which gifts are most valuable in the church? *Wrong question!* Paul concludes. All the various gifts in the church work together to create one well-functioning body. If you take any out, or if you make the whole body just one part, you ruin the beauty, not only of the whole, but of all the individual parts as well. They are only beautiful when they complement one another and work together. The same is true when it comes to our jobs in society. None of them stand alone. All of them are ordered by God to create one well-functioning body, and the roles of all of us complement and support one another. They all work together to make society work.

IT ALL COMES DOWN TO DEPLOYMENT

If that's true, then there's no logical formula you can run to tell you what job is most valuable and therefore what you should spend your life doing. We shouldn't all be pastors, and we shouldn't all be police officers either. So how does it all get determined? Simple. The King deploys us as he wills. He puts us where we will serve his purposes best. Some he deploys as pastors and missionaries; others he deploys as teachers and business-people. Ultimately, it is up to him. Therefore, don't resent it too deeply if you find yourself in a place you'd rather not be. This is where the King has deployed you, and he has reasons for doing so. Maybe he'll deploy you to do something else later. You may be learning skills now that will make you more effective in your next deployment. What matters is doing the work your King has given you to do—and doing it well.

Consider the story of Joseph recorded in the book of Genesis. Do you really think Joseph wanted to be working in the house of Potiphar, even after Potiphar appointed him to be in charge of the entire household? No! He'd been sold into slavery by his brothers. He really wanted to be back home with his father. Yet he served faithfully where he was because he knew he was ulti-mately rendering service to God, not to Potiphar.

Joseph's faithfulness in this way is even more amazing when Potiphar has him thrown into prison. Even while imprisoned, Joseph faithfully carried out the work that was given to him. Why? Because he was working in the name of God. So be encouraged. Maybe the current assignment your King has given you is not what you would have chosen for yourself. That's fine.

Consider yourself privileged and blessed beyond measure even to be in his service at all. Trust him. Trust his judgment. Trust his wisdom in how he is using you. Serve him with everything you are, wherever he has placed you.

How do you figure out where God is deploying you? After all, it's not as if a high-priority e-mail shows up from heaven with the subject line "Your Next Job." Sure, it may be simple to look down and say about the job you're in right now, "This is where God has deployed me for this season." The harder question is to look forward and ask, "Where is God deploying me for the *next season*?" — whether that season starts next decade or next year or tomorrow.

Again, many books have been written about the topic of discerning God's will. We won't take the time to say everything that could be said. But we can say it's both simpler and more complex than many Christians think. It's simpler because discerning God's will really comes down to what you *want* to do, multiplied by what you are *gifted* to do, multiplied by what opportunities are *available* to you right now. You don't have to put out a fleece or wait for a liver shiver or try to interpret signs. God hasn't hidden his will from you, sending you out on some sort of sick scavenger hunt. No, it really is simply a matter of lining up desire, gifting, and opportunity. On the other hand, thinking it through carefully can be more complicated than getting a "sign in the sky"! It requires you to think, pray, and seek godly counsel. It requires you to vet your desires and make sure they're not sinful in some way, to be honest about your gifts and abilities, and to find contentment in that season when what you want to do simply isn't available.

There's nothing wrong with looking ahead, dreaming about future possibilities, and doing the hard thinking about where God might intend to deploy you next. If you see a job that lines up with your gifts and abilities, is available to you, and is something you want to do, reread chapter 5 in this book and go for it! If not, that's the point at which it becomes crucial for you to trust that King Jesus has you where he has you for good reasons. And his reasons are *always* good.

CONCLUSION

So back to the question with which we started: Is your job less valuable than your pastor's job? Well, no — not any more than the heart is less valuable than the brain, or the infantryman is less valuable than the cavalryman. If that's true, then "value" really doesn't have much to do with it at all. It comes down to *calling*. What has God called you to do? In other words, what has he given you desire and ability and opportunity to do? Yes, God calls some people into full-time ministry in the local church, and that is a noble calling. He calls others to be lawyers and doctors and soldiers and politicians and salespeople and managers, and those are noble callings too, because they all work together to create a well-functioning society.

What has God called you to do? What do you want to do, and what has God given you ability and opportunity to do? We need to be asking those questions rather than trying to run some equation that will tell us, "The most valuable job on the planet is *X*." No, the point is not value. The point is whether you are doing what God has called you to do — and whether you are doing it well.

1. Read and Reflect: Matthew 20:1 – 16; Romans 12:3 – 8; 1 Corinthians 12:12 – 27

2. Have you ever felt more valuable or less valuable than those in full-time Christian ministry? What makes you feel this way?

3. Walk through the logic of this chapter. Why is thinking that your job is more valuable or less valuable than another job a bad way to think about service to the King?

4. What are the ways you assign value to various jobs? Is it by money, power, fame? What is the biblical way to think about differences in jobs?

5. Have you ever thought about pursuing full-time ministry? Why or why not? Evaluate your motives with another person.

6. If you are a pastor, how can you gain a greater passion for building up the workers in your church? How can you gain greater skills for this important task?

DEFINING SUCCESS

You work for the King. No matter your company or compensation, you work for King Jesus. That's the idea we've been hammering home throughout this book, and once you start conceiving of your job in those terms, the ramifications are enormous. All of a sudden, you realize your job can't provide for you everything the world says it can. It can't give you an identity or ultimate purpose or meaning. Your work will not and cannot fully satisfy you. When you work for Jesus, the allure of making your job the object of your worship fades.

Not only that, but you also realize it just won't do simply to slog through your workday, telling yourself it doesn't really matter, doing a mediocre job, treating your coworkers with indifference or disdain, and generally just banging through the hours so you can get away. Once you realize you work for Jesus, you also realize he has put you in your job for a reason, and therefore idleness in your work — being blind to God's purposes and thus not caring about your job — is no longer an option.

No idolatry of work. No idleness in work. Rather, we aim to be faithful to the King, who put us where we are. When we work for Jesus, the very definition of what it means to succeed changes. The world has all kinds of ideas about how to measure success. Money is one way. "He who dies with the most toys wins," goes the old saying. Power is another measurement. The one who accrues over a lifetime the most influence over people—*that's* a successful person. Even tangible impact can be a measurement. Steve Jobs and his information revolution defined success, according to that way of thinking. For some, simple survival is success. If there's food on the table, a roof over the head, a college fund for the kids, and an occasional vacation, then we are living a successful life.

If you've tracked with us throughout this book, you may already be able to see why none of those definitions of success really cut it for a Christian. Each in its own way betrays a mind that is either making too much or too little of our work. For a Christian, though, the definition of success really has little to do with any of those things—money, power, influence, change, a respectable standard of living. Instead, success is defined as *faithfulness*—doing whatever we do with sincerity of heart because we know the King is watching. Maybe your work will bring a lot of money—that's great! Maybe it will bring power or influence—that's great! Maybe it will change the world. Maybe it will give your family a respectable standard of living. Yes, maybe. Or maybe not. Ultimately, none of those things make you a success.

What makes you a success is being able to stand before King Jesus one day and say, "Lord, where you deployed me, I served well. I gave it my all. I worked at it with all my heart because I was working for you, not for human masters."

When that becomes your goal, it is enormously freeing because you no longer have to define success on the world's terms; you define it on Jesus' terms. It frees you from trying to find success by comparing yourself to others. Instead, success is defined simply by giving your all for King Jesus. You may not be the most talented person on the planet. Perhaps you're a one- or two-talent person instead of a five-talent person. So what? Your King has made you who you are. He has deployed you to work where he wants you to work, and your job is to be faithful to him, to give your all with everything he has given you. Many Christians struggle daily with perfectionism and comparison, even with envy. If that's you, then hear God's gracious, freeing call to faithfulness rather than to perfection. Working for the King frees us from the tyranny of comparing ourselves to others in order to feel good about ourselves.

Working for Jesus also frees us from measuring success by the results we get. Instead, we define success simply by working well and trusting God with the outcome. Proverbs 16 is one of the most important passages of Scripture to read, especially if you're a driven, results-oriented person. Read through that chapter and look at the verbs it uses for what *we* do. These proverbs tell us that humans make plans (16:1, 9), evaluate their ways (16:2), and cast lots (16:33). But look at what *the Lord* does. He provides the answer (16:1), weighs people's motives (16:2), establishes their plans and their steps (16:3, 9), works out everything (16:4), and is in control of every decision (16:33). We may plan and scheme and work, but the outcome is God's to determine. What a wonderfully freeing truth that is! The God of the universe, the God who loved me and gave his own Son for me, holds in his powerful hands even the results of my work. If I succeed, he has decided to let me succeed. If I fail, then that, too, he has decided. I can trust that, whatever the outcome, "in all things God works for the good of those who love him" (Romans 8:28). Outcomes simply are not in our hands. We work hard and smart. We work with all our heart. And we trust God with the results. We push hard on the plow, but always with an open hand.

Working for Jesus frees us from having to measure success by immediate rewards. The fruits of hard labor that we receive in this life are great. But no matter how much joy we may take in the rewards of a job well done, as Christians we know that our greatest rewards will only come to us when we stand before Jesus—and unlike anything this world affords, those rewards will never spoil or fade. That's exactly the kind of anchor for the soul that lets us work with all our heart, love God, and love others in our workplaces without fear of what those things might do to our career track. We get to give it our all, and we don't have to worry about the final score. Why? Because no matter what the score is at the end of this world, we know we've already won in the next one. Our reward is waiting for us in the nail-scarred hands of the One who has already completed his work.

After reading this book, we hope you can see how focusing your mind on the truth that you work for Jesus brings immense freedom in your job. Work is no longer a crushing tyranny that demands our worship or a grinding schlep that leaves us feeling drained, used, and purposeless. How could it be, when our King's work has already won for us the most important things in the universe? Because of Jesus' work on the cross on our behalf, because he lives and reigns right now, we have identity, belonging, love, acceptance, forgiveness, adoption, justification, and reward. It is all ours for all eternity. Because that's true, we are gloriously freed from having to pursue those things (or, rather, cheap imitations of them) through our work. Do you see? We don't need our work to provide an identity for us. We already have an identity in Christ. We don't need it to give us a place to belong. We already have been adopted by God because of Jesus, and we belong to his redeemed family. We don't need work to make us loved or liked or accepted, nor do we need it to prove to ourselves that we're worthwhile. Why? Because all of that has already been secured for us by Jesus!

So where does that leave our work? What role does that leave for it to play in our lives? Simple. It leaves our work liberated from the impossible demand to provide something for us that it was never meant to provide and from the excuse that it doesn't matter, and we are set free to live lives of joyful, heartfelt service to our King!

1. Read and Reflect: Proverbs 16; Romans 8:28

2. Summarize the big idea of this book. How does it challenge your view of success?

3. Write your job description — from God's perspective.

4. What worldly temptations are you most susceptible to?

5. How would you describe the ways that working for King Jesus give you purpose and meaning in your job?

ACKNOWLEDGMENTS

A bove all, we praise God for his grace in giving us the interest, vision, and energy for writing this book. This book is born out of our own questions, angst, and struggles in the workplace, and out of our searching the Scriptures for help.

There are so many people God has used to shape our thinking and to encourage us in faithfulness. Special thanks to Matt Aiello and Ashok Nachnani, two brothers whose godly wisdom and counsel have been a huge practical encouragement.

We have also been blessed by our own churches—Third Avenue Baptist Church in Louisville (Greg) and Capitol Hill Baptist Church in Washington, DC (Seb). We praise God for these faithful saints, and we pray that the partnership between these two churches will continue to grow in fruitfulness for many years.

To Mark Dever, thank you for your commitment to faithful expositional preaching and application and for your determination to teach those skills to others. And thank you to other brothers who have shaped our thinking as well. Mike Gilbart-Smith, Andrew Nichols, Jonathan Leeman, Jamie Dunlop, Josh Morrell, Scott Croft, and Bob Tucker have been great thought partners. Ryan Townsend, Jason Townsend, Gus Pritchard,

Justin Wredberg, and Corby Megorden have been wonderful encouragers, as have the teams at Marketplace One and at Redeemer Presbyterian Church's Ei Forum.

Special thanks to Josh Trent, who wrote the study questions at the end of each chapter and who has been a big encouragement to press on throughout this project.

I (Seb) especially want to thank my great partners in business over the years—Duncan Rein, Brian Fujito, and David Lam—who helped refine my thinking and who know only too well what a work in progress I am when it comes to bringing the gospel to bear on my work. I'm also thankful to my coworkers at Christianity.com and Razoo and to the investment teams at Legatum and FiveStreet, and especially to Tom Holton, who had faith in two twentysomethings and who is a model of faithful service to the King.

Lastly, we both want to thank (respectively, of course!) our most cherished partners in this project and in the journey of life. To our awesome wives, Nikki Traeger and Moriah Gilbert, a million thank yous! You both give so much and receive so little in loving such imperfect men. Through your love, your support, and your encouragement—in your roles as wives, mothers, church members, friends, and encouragers—you show truly and clearly what it means to "work for the King." We love you so, so much!

FIVE PRACTICES TO HELP YOU LIVE OUT THE GOSPEL AT WORK

Over the years, I (Seb) have adopted five practices to help me in my struggle to live out the gospel at work. While you might not sign up for all of these (or any of them), I encourage you to think about how you can build routines into your life to help you grow in faithfulness and fruitfulness.

TIME WITH JESUS: BE IN THE WORD AND PRAYER DAILY

One of the key ways to grow as Christians is to go straight to the source, God's Word. Romans 12:2 urges, "Be transformed by the renewing of your mind"—and regular time in the Word is great for this. I like to think of spending time in the Word as resembling what happens with a coffee percolator. If you run water through coffee grounds, dark coffee comes out. If you keep running new water through those same grounds, what comes out will get lighter and lighter. When you let the Word run through you, your heart is changed, and more Christlikeness comes out of you.

For those of you in the marketplace, I suggest you read a chapter of Proverbs every day. Its thirty-one chapters track with the thirty or thirty-one days of the average month. You always know which chapter to read based on the day of the month. By my count, more than 150 proverbs relate to the workplace, and so you'll find that as your workday unfolds, you'll call them to mind often. This Bible book is rich in application as it lays out what godly wisdom looks like in the life of the Christian. Consider this small sampling from Proverbs 16:

- "Kings take pleasure in honest lips; they value the one who speaks what is right" (16:13).
- "Honest scales and balances belong to the LORD; all the weights in the bag are of his making" (16:11).
- "Better a patient person than a warrior, one with self-control than one who takes a city" (16:32).

I also encourage you to pray through your calendar, your to-do list, and your workplace relationships every day. Before you start the day, pause for a few minutes to pray through the various meetings, memos, e-mails, phone calls, and interactions you'll have. Pray for humility, grace, and patience. Pray that you'll be worshipful, thanking the Lord for the job and the opportunities to do good works for the praise of his glory. Pray that you'll be gracious in difficult relationships. Pray that you will serve your boss and customers well, as working for the Lord.

Finally, if you are feeling anxious about or preoccupied with the future, go on a long walk or take a journal to the nearest coffee shop. Remind yourself of what God has saved you from—your sin—and what he has saved you to—new and eternal life. Remember all the ways that God has proven trustworthy in the past. Trace out how your specific anxiety is dispelled in light of the gospel. Let Jesus be the anchor of your trust. I know I need to do this every few months to address the struggle to make an idol of work or to be idle in it.

BELONG: ATTEND AND BE ACTIVELY INVOLVED IN A LOCAL CHURCH

If you are going to take off as a disciple, you need two wings — your own personal time of reading the Bible and prayer is one, and your local church is the other. God has graciously called us to gather in local churches where we can worship God, hear the truths of his Word proclaimed, and remind each other of God's faithfulness — where we can walk through life and be known by others. Gathering to build up others who may not have the same education, ethnicity, or experiences we have is a great reminder that we are not to measure success by the world's standards.

ACCOUNTABILITY: BE HONEST ABOUT YOUR LIFE WITH OTHERS

Accountability relationships help you fight against the patterns of this world and the ways they affect your thinking and practices. I do this by meeting with a friend from church biweekly to go through the four key spheres of life. We schedule the same time every week. If we miss a week, we just pick back up the next week. We meet at a coffee shop for thirty to forty-five minutes to talk through these key areas of our lives: personal discipleship, relationships (marriage and parenting, if applicable), ministry, and work. We each take ten minutes and think about these areas in terms of how our past weeks went and what our goals are for the upcoming week. We go over each of these with the other person and give them permission to ask us hard questions about any of them. Typically, there is one area on which we spend the majority of our time, thinking about it from a biblical perspective. For example, my accountability partner was trying to think through how to best disciple his young children. Over the course of a few weeks as we reflected on the Bible's message about the priority of this, he tried different strategies and gleaned insights from different books until he found what seemed to work best for him.

This approach is also especially helpful if you struggle to do *good* work. Your accountability partner can help you fight for faithfulness by developing good work habits: arriving at the same time each morning, fighting distractions at the office, and remembering that good work is the fruit of *faithful* work. Beyond all that, the key truth to realize is that this is a battle for intrinsic motivation, a battle for your heart. Your accountability partner can help you gauge your heart.

REVIEW: DO PERIODIC ASSIGNMENT REVIEWS

I recommend doing an assignment review periodically. You can do this alone as part of a daily prayer time, or you can do it with a friend or spouse. By recalibrating your life on a semi-regular basis, you can catch bad habits or sin patterns early and refocus your efforts on faithfulness and fruitfulness. I also review my schedule weekly with my wife, and every few months I thoroughly review all the big things I give my time and attention to so I can think through the best way to organize them in order to be faithful in my assignments. I try to think through my ideal schedule for doing what I think God is calling me to do during a given season. For me, seasons seem to be every six months or so, as the schedules of my wife, children, church, and work seem to adjust about that often. For example, my current season of life makes it difficult to have as much time for casual friendships as in other seasons. So, with the blessing of my wife, I've blocked off Tuesday nights — post-dinner, post-kids to bed, post-catch-up with my wife—from 9:00 to 10:30 to reengage with any friends I can corral to sit in the backyard around the fire pit. Some nights it's just me and one friend, while other nights four or five friends show up.

The other benefit of a periodic assignment review is that over time you'll learn how you are wired and which schedule and lifestyle fit best with your unique wiring. For example, over the years, I've realized I can handle long hours of work—as long as they are consistent. It's actually harder for me to order my life—regardless of the number of hours I need to work—if the hours and travel required are inconsistent. Knowing this motivates me to build more regularity into my schedule.

RETREAT: TAKE TIME TO GET AWAY

One of the great joys of my life is my wife, Nikki. Our marriage has benefited from our biannual marriage retreats, which we schedule around our anniversary (December 31, so it's pretty easy for us) and the middle of the year. We highly value these getaways and make sure we budget for them. While the times are always special and memorable, they're not necessarily expensive or luxurious. Depending on the length of time that our extended family (bless them!) is willing and able to watch our kids, we spend one to two nights away.

Our goal is to relax, enjoy one another, and talk about our lives. Our agenda is to have fun and to have three long conversations—one to review the past six months (and we go month by month, writing down significant memories and then summarizing them in themes); one to talk about our relationship, with topics ranging from communication, to intimacy, to how each of us is doing spiritually, to the ways we've been encouraging each other, to how our schedules are affecting our marriage; and one to talk about the next six months as we think about our relationships with our children, our church friends, and our extended family; the way our schedules are shaping up; the state of our finances; and our hopes and dreams for our future. We use a marriage retreat document to guide these conversations. Obviously, these wide-ranging topics can go in a lot of directions. In a fast-paced world, setting aside time every six months to talk with the person specially chosen by God to help me has been a great investment in our lives.

In addition to a biannual marriage retreat, I also go on an annual ManTreat. The name should tell you two things: (1) I have an awesome wife to let me do this, and (2) it's a time for me to go away with three or four of my best friends (including Greg, the coauthor of this book). We obviously have a ton of fun on the trip, but, we also have very intentional conversations. Our schedule is pretty simple: play, eat, talk informally, and rest during the day; then talk deliberately at night (usually from about 9:00 p.m. to 2:00 a.m.).

We try to schedule three nights away, and each night we have a conversation around a theme: family/parenting, church/ministry, and work/future. Each guy is on the hot seat for an hour per topic. They share about their life in that particular area and ask us questions ("Hey, what are you all doing for schooling, and why?"). We use the rest of the time to ask questions we might have ("Last year you said you were going to get your budget under control. How's that going? What steps have you taken? How has your heart been losing its grip on money?"). The goal of the retreat is to encourage each other and critique our lives, all with the goal of building each other up to be faithful disciples who have multiple assignments. I encourage you, if this is at all possible for you, to find two to four other people to get away with annually for some amount of time. My high school baseball coach once told me that the Christian life is a marathon and not a sprint. We need to have partners to help us finish the race well.